LOVER RELATIONSHIPS AND KARMA

LOVER RELATIONSHIPS AND KARMA

Dr Patricia Sherwood

Cover: Gustav Klimt, 1909, The Kiss

Lover relationships and karma
Dr Patricia Sherwood
Email : info@sophiacollege.com
Copyright 2016 Patricia Sherwood

All rights reserved. No part of this book may be reproduced in any form or by any means, electronic or mechanical, including photocopying, recording, or by any information storage and retrieval system without written permission from the publisher.

The case study examples do not refer to any one person or couple but are composite experiences that are typical of this type of relationship.

National Library of Australia Cataloguing-in-Publication entry

Creator: Sherwood, Patricia, author.

Title: Lover relationships and karma / Patricia Sherwood.

ISBN: 9780987614308 (paperback)

Subjects: Mate selection. Man-woman relationships. Interpersonal relations--Psychic aspects. Marriage counseling. Self-actualization (Psychology) Spirituality. Karma.

Printed & Channel Distribution

Lightning Source | Ingram (USA/UK/EUROPE/AUS)

Dedication

To Janet for her enduring colleagueship, her deep and profound understanding of this energetic model of therapy and for her unwavering support in developing this model of therapy and not least, for editing so many of my publications. Her encouragement and support for my work is beyond measure and deeply and profoundly appreciated. An old friend over many lifetimes and many places.

Forward

This book is for all lovers who believe that they had found their life-partner, their soul mate, the partner of their dreams and the promise of enduring love. While it focuses on passionate lovers, the core experiences, although less intense are realities for all who have fallen in love with whom they believe is their life partner.

It explores the deep interplay of karmas in the human body, mind and feeling life to illustrate how love relationships are born, develop and either flourish or die. It empowers the reader to understand that they are not a powerless victim of karma but equips them with the knowledge of how karma works through the human body, soul and mind. It uncovers karmic patterns and processes and identifies how they can take action to create skilful karmic outcomes in their intimate relationships.

These findings are grounded in over 10,000 hours of holistic clinical counselling work revealing the deepest karmic patterns that shape our lives and relationships. They elucidate a depth of human relationship experience rarely spoken of or revealed. They expose the core challenges of intimate relationships and offer a depth of understanding of self, relationships and the cycles of karma manifest through love relationships and particularly obvious in passionate lover relationships.

Contents

Chapter 1: The karmic meeting: fulfilling the dream   1

Chapter 2: The karmas of passion: fusing together   23

Chapter 3: Karmic differences: challenges to intimacy   39

Chapter 4: Childhood shadow karmas: tearing love apart   67

Chapter 5: Dying in relationship: dark shadow karmas   89

Chapter 6: The aftermath karmas: grief, despair and hatred   123

Chapter 7: The karmas of light and darkness in relationships   141

Chapter 1

The karmic meeting: fulfilling the dream

Dicksee, Frank (1903) *The Belle Dame sans Merci*

> We cannot anticipate in advance how anyone will respond when they first rub elbows with Eros' malady of passion and madness. Eros arrives on a wing of a devious angel to take control of our body, encapsulate our mind and seize command over the quality of our life. In its purest manifestation, romantic love guarantees to rip us asunder, because we are unwittingly dispossessed of our precious sense of self-control.

– Oldster, K., *Dead Toad Scrolls*
www.goodreads.com/quotes/tag/passionate-love

1. The Dream

The dream within the heart and soul of adults seeking an intimate relationship is driven by the desire for union with another adult that embraces body, heart and mind; a connectedness in which each person feels profoundly understood and unconditionally accepted as a human being worth loving. In this process, they experience becoming profoundly important and precious to another person. Intimate passionate love has been the undying quest of human beings in western cultures and has been immortalised in movies, literature and the arts. Elizabeth Barrett Browning (1850) captures this experience of being in intimate love in her remarkable love sonnets:

> How do I love thee? Let me count the ways.
> I love thee to the depth and breadth and height
> My soul can reach, when feeling out of sight
> For the ends of being and ideal grace.
> I love thee to the level of every day's
> Most quiet need, by sun and candle-light.
> I love thee freely, as men strive for right.
> I love thee purely, as they turn from praise.
> I love thee with the passion put to use
> In my old griefs, and with my childhood's faith.
> I love thee with a love I seemed to lose
> With my lost saints. I love thee with the breath,
> Smiles, tears, of all my life; and, if God choose,
> I shall but love thee better after death.

Coupled with a culture of romantic love that elevates passion, romance and sensuality as ideals, falling in love is a much sought after experience. In western culture, planned intimate relationships based on practical considerations have been upstaged by the search for one's soul mate, passionate love at first sight, and love that is consuming. Such love has been variously described as romantic love, extreme love, infatuation and "limerence". Passionate love is marked by "limerence," a term used to describe a disconnection from daily life and an elevation to almost other worldly experience of intensity and obsession with the loved one (Tennov,1979). It is love that begins with a lightning bolt full of radiant promise and hope. This is what one has been waiting for all of one's life. It is that inescapable heartthrob, with intense extraordinary emotions and intrusive thoughts towards the beloved. This consuming desire can strike at any age, any time and in any place. For some people it occurs rarely or not at all, while for others several times in their lifetime. The moment when passionate love strikes, there is only one person in the world other than oneself, for all energy is focused upon the loved one. When it occurs, it is transformative and there is a shift in daily consciousness often causing disruptions in one's appetite, sleeping patterns, sense of time and routine activities.

Experiences of passionate love

These experiences are identified by Stundberg (2015) who researched how lovers' experience intense love relationships in the USA. He revealed core themes in human experiences of passionate love, particularly in the western cultures.

Dynamic connection

There is a vibrant energy of connectedness experienced as an insurmountably attractive call, bringing one another together like opposite magnetic poles. Often it is described as electric, as it causes bodily sensations. It is a driven impulse to be together and choice feels to be minimal. This love has a life of its own and to resist is anguishing and almost impossible. Body, mind and spirit want to be fused, interpenetrated and exalted to a place beyond the aloneness of the day-to-day grind of the human condition. The connection is so strong that time disappears and one's priorities are radically altered and centred around the beloved one. There is also the sense of being able to share deeply with this person and to expose oneself to this person. There is the immediate feeling of familiarity with this person, as though one has known them before, a sense of "deja-vous."

Intense emotions

All feelings are heightened but especially feelings of excitement, adventure, contentment, happiness, joy, warmth and positivity that are magnified beyond normal experience. Emotions could be easily described a euphoric as though one is living an exalted sense of feeling that is only available because of the beloved one. These intense feelings drive one compulsively to focus upon the beloved one. Emotions are so intense that feeling "weak at the knees", having a "fluttering heart", "churning stomach" or "butterflies" are all part of the excitement, uniqueness and intensity of the experience.

Mental absorption

Pre-occupation with the newfound lover is typical of this experience, so one often feels so overwhelmed and consumed by the thoughts of their beloved that it is difficult to focus on mundane activities. All of one's thoughts focus upon the lover in a possessive and often irrational way. Even when there are signs that the lover is dangerous, this awareness is likely to be blotted out and flooded by the attractive thoughts and feelings which over-ride otherwise clear judgments that would caution one and recommend avoidance. It is not surprising that at these times people talk about being "madly in love" or "blinded by love". This is not an experience based upon measured reflective thought. Rather, it is an experience of such emotional intensity that the emotional maelstrom that it generates, often clouds the lovers' judgments with desire.

Extraordinary nature of this extreme love connection.

Other core aspects to these types of passionate love relationships are the belief that this is a soul-mate connection, something preordained in the universe, a meeting divined in the heavens for two persons, complementary in every way. There is the experience of feeling one has found one's other half, that finally one can be complete and whole, and that the intimacy embraces all of the body, mind and spirit. It has been described as knowing what one another is thinking, tuning in to each other's needs, and a soul kinship in which we each understand the other without words. "We are made for each other" is the description of many passionate lovers. At times, it has a mystical or religious quality for those who experience it, beyond the realm of ordinary romantic relationships (Stundberg, 2015). It is at these moments, that one perceives all that is best in their lover. One is inspired by a vision of the potential of the union and of the sense of embracing acceptance of one another.

> *"At the very heart of our experience of being human, each of us has an intuitive sense of the value of unconditional love. We discover great joy when we can love without reservation, suspending judgments and opening fully to the vivid reality of another's being. And we usually feel most loved when others recognize and respond to us wholeheartedly. Unconditional love has tremendous power, activating a larger energy, which connects us with the vastness and profundity of what it is to be human. This energy is the energy of the heart." (Welwood, J., 1985, p. 33)*

Biology of passionate love

Passionate love is also a profoundly driven biological experience. All lovers know this to be true and science has recently revealed an elaborate chain of bodily hormonal reactions that fuel the love experience. There are three phases in this biologically driven process:

1. Sexual desire

Initially the sexual desire is instigated by the sexual hormones in the body and this is very specifically driven by each person's response to the body language of the other as well as the person's smell, appearance and touch. Estrogen and testosterone are the basic hormones that drive sexual desire but at an energetic level, more is happening (Fisher, 2004).

Lover relationships and karma

There needs to be a match between the sexuality of the lovers, which is driven by energetic familiarity, and complementarity. As we all know, there are certain persons, regardless of how much we like them, who simply could not be our lovers. In karmic terms, the more intense the desire, the more intense the karmas. That essentially means that intense passion can only be experienced with persons with whom one has profound energetic familiarity. We have known them in other days and times.

2. The attraction

The "falling in love" or attraction is fuelled by adrenaline which gives us a euphoric sense in the meeting, together with the serotonin which diverts our mind to our lover, and bonds us in our desires to our lover. It causes us to focus on our lover, to the exclusion of other persons and to become pre-occupied with being physically proximate to our lover.

Attraction and the passion are driven by the chemical hormones of adrenaline, dopamine and serotonin. They profoundly affect our bodily processes including a significant surge in energy, a decrease in hunger and a decline in the need for sleep. The bodily processes are focused on the object of desire. In particular, serotonin produces the exciting feelings of being in love, and channels the chemical pathways in the brain to focus and concentrate upon the beloved. There is an increase in adrenalin and cortisol, which contribute to strong feelings of alertness around your lover (Fisher, 2004).

MRI's reveal that the minds of both males and females in love, have large spikes of the neurotransmitter dopamine. These hormones stimulate sensations of pleasure and contentment in the body, exalting the lovers at a sensory level, so that qualities of happiness and joy which are often elusive in day-to-day life, or short term, are now are readily accessible for longer periods of time (Fisher, 2004).

3. Attachment

Attachment is the biological process of wanting to "pair up," to create the bonding that takes a couple to deeper levels including reproducing. This is driven by oxytocin also known as the "cuddle hormone," which is released abundantly when men and women orgasm, and which cements the physical attachment between the lovers. In passionate relationships, the more frequent the sex, the more intense the chemical bonding between the partners. Oxytocin also enhances the ability of lovers to interpret cues from each other's eyes and so strengthens and enhances couple communication and social bonding. In addition, vasopressin is released in abundance following sex and this chemical further promotes couple bonding. There is a direct positive correlation between vasopressin levels and interpersonal functioning, spousal support, attachment security, relationship maintenance and positive communication (*Why we fall in love* :http://examinedexistence.com/why-we-fall-in-love-the-science-of-love/ accessed 31-8-16).

Lover relationships and karma

Karmic energies and passionate love

While biochemistry describes some pathways for physical experience and connectedness, within passionate love relationships, we need to move to the energetic realms of karma to deeply understand the phenomena. Karma is the outworking in the present moment, of energetic patterns created by ours and others' intentions and actions in these past meetings. The power of the human will and the associated thoughts have profound effects on creating realities that go on to manifest in the physical realms. Karma can be basically described metaphorically as throwing a handful of marbles in a particular direction through a conscious intention and/or action. The more focused the intention, the greater the velocity with which the thought marbles travel. Some of these thought marbles extinguish their velocity in a single life-time, but others travel through several lifetimes. These stored karmic patterns are yet to be discovered in empirical science, but in human experience they have been extensively documented in many diverse cultural experiences. In western cultures, several therapists have explored these dimensions of the human psyche including the pioneer British psychiatrist, Arthur Guirdham in 1978. Other past life regressionists who have published include Roger Woolger (1988, 2006, 2004), Lawton (2008), Henry Bolduc (2016) and Fenwick and Fenwick (2001).

These therapists primarily use hypnosis or a trance state of mental activity to regress clients. I do not use this process but rather an active, alert, fully aware process whereby the client steps into the feeling of contracted breathing in a particular part of the body when the client recounts a traumatic experience in their life today, which they wish to heal and transform. They become the shape of the contraction with their whole body and in the process they will spontaneously, and in full alert, aware consciousness recall earlier experiences from childhood, or previous lives that underlie the presenting issue for which they have come to therapy (Sherwood, 2007). I have observed that in this process, it appears likely that the body cells in the DNA carry vast stores of information, emotional and mental, that we have only just begun to explore and access. This body cell memory phenomenon is further elucidated by Rothschild (2011) in her seminal collection of articles, *The Body Remembers*.

It is important to be aware that time is an illusion and the past, present and future all co-exist in the same moment: the present. Meetings with a lover are not for the first time. Hence, people often describe the experience as "déjà-vu", finding a lost "soul-mate" and the like. All experiences with that lover are concurrent in the present moment. As quantum physics demonstrates, all energy patterns co-exist in the present moment regardless of where they are located in our models of time. This is well demonstrated in the movie: *What the bleep do we know.* (2004), which graphically as well as scientifically presents a very convincing case.

The 4-fold, anthroposphically based holistic model used to elucidate karmic patterns in relationships

This model of psychotherapy assumes that a human being is an interrelated energetic system and in particular, that mind, body, and spirit are not separate entities, but rather inextricably connected. All experiences have energetic resonances in the cellular structures of the body. Developed by Steiner, this model of a human being includes firstly, the physical body, secondly, the etheric or life force, akin to the chi or pranic force in eastern medicine and thirdly, the astrality or trauma system which relates to the reptilian brain which is in a flight/fight response mode and is driven by fear, aversion and desire. Finally, the fourth part of the model, which Steiner refers to as the "I" or the "I am "is connected to the higher order thinking capacities of will, insight, creativity, motivation and reflection, all essentially frontal lobe activities. The "I" has the capacity to link us to the transpersonal world and can be termed the human spirit and is easily tracked by the flow of the breath in the body (Steiner, 1994). The "I" also provides the spiritual energy that underlines our ethics and morals, the quality of which, depend on the level of the "I"s connection to the spiritual world (Steiner, 1999). The relationship between these four bodies is critical to physical, emotional, mental and spiritual health. No part of the human being functions independently. All of the four bodies are intricately connected. Each body is separated from the other by a sheath, known in Hindu psychology as a "kosha" (Sachedeva, 2012). The number of bodies and sheaths vary in different models of a human being, but in Steiner's model, there are four sheaths and associated bodies.

These four bodies are represented diagrammatically below:

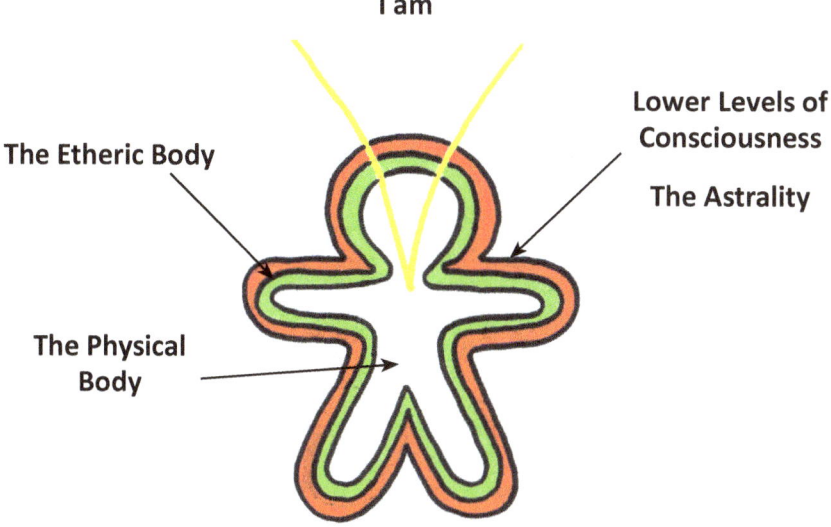

Diagram 1: Outline of the four-fold model.

The physical body

The physical body is seen as the map of the mind and feeling states and is that part of our experience that can be clearly touched and observed. It reflects our feeling life and when experiencing emotional intensity, contractions in the breathing result in tensions or stresses in different parts of the body. These contractions are a result of the etheric or life-force without which the physical body would simply return to the mineral kingdom from which it has been formed (Steiner, 1994).

The etheric or life-force

Interpenetrating the physical body is what Steiner termed the ether body, the etheric or the life body. In China, it is akin to the chi, in India it is akin to the pranic body. It is a template on a more subtle vibration, of the physical body and is responsible for the life and health of the physical body, sending the energy needed to repair, nourish and maintain life processes of breathing, reproduction, digestion and sleeping cycles (Steiner: 1999). The shape and wellbeing of our body's organs depend on this force and its degree of vitality. While constitutionally people vary in the strength of the etheric, good rhythmical habits of eating, sleeping, exercising, and spending time in nature strengthen this body. Pollution of air, water, food, and electromagnetic radiation weaken it and consequently weaken the vitality of the physical body.

The lower layers of mind consciousness: astrality ("the trauma system"/flight/fight responses.

The astrality is described by Steiner (1994) as embracing the basic animal instincts, impulses, sensations and passion. It has the capacity to bring thinking into its service to process and shape the sensory experiences. Here, in the astral body, all the vibrational patterns of our sensory experiences, positive and negative are stored. The astral body holds the imprints of all our experiences that are stored in layers of 7 years. The closest layer is contemporary experience, and the layers of stored experience go back through childhood and into previous lifetimes. It is essentially the storehouse of all our sensory experiences, most of which are unconscious unless triggered by environmental stimuli in the current life. These patterns of experience, Sherwood terms imprints (2004:20). Many of our defence mechanisms merge out of our struggle to survive and avoid pain on the astral level. These defence mechanisms result in many aspects of experience being cut off, denied and suppressed. Buried astral experiences often run the life through the unconscious. This trauma system lacks integration with the self system or "I" and consequently is responsible for most of our intimate relationship problems. Very often couples are in conflict over seemingly trivial things, but underpinning these are deep patterns of karmic hurt that go far beyond even childhood woundings, into other life times of experience with the lover.

The relationship between the etheric and astrality is critical, for the etheric acts as a buffer between the physical body and astral experiences. If the etheric is robust in both couples, it minimises the potential conflict sites between lovers. It provides a padding, so to speak between one's traumas and one's physical body. This is clearly understood in family systems in an experiential manner. We are aware that most arguments and conflicts arise in the evening or when someone is tired, exhausted or energetically depleted. These conditions thin the etheric sheath and reduce its capacity to insulate trauma in the astral body, so that it is insulated from the physical body.

The "I am" or "I": integrated self: insight, self-awareness, will, motivation.

In this model, the reflective, integrated self system of human consciousness, is referred to as the "I am" or the "I". It is the individualised level of consciousness. At the higher levels of consciousness, it becomes the connection to the highest resources of the human spirit. It is the self-aware human consciousness. The "I" also carries the essence of each unique human being that needs to be manifested in each person's life. This "I am" also comprises the integrated self of each human being and captures our individuality or that part of ourselves which represents the best of who we can be.

Psychological health and well being depend on the capacity of people to insert their "I am" into their experiences and to integrate and process all experiences in a meaningful way so that no experience remains cut-off, denied, or repressed (Sherwood, 2004). If this does not occur, then one's life remains driven by the astrality or the trauma system, which is characterised by aversions and desires, rather than by skilful means. The stronger the "I am", the stronger the ability of a person to access the part of the "I" that connects them with spiritual resources. These resources are invoked through positive experiences, images and archetypes in the spiritual worlds, the human worlds or the physical worlds. The "I" creates connectedness and as such enables us to invoke other resources in the world and the universe, to strengthen and enlarge our problem solving capacities, our insight, our vision and our decision-making capacity. Steiner (1999) also clearly connects the highest levels of the "I" with the transpersonal spiritual world.

Steiner (1999, pp39-40) also describes the relationship between the physical, etheric and astral bodies and "I", as dynamic, each interpenetrating the other:

> *"The physical body would fall apart if the etheric body did not hold it together. The etheric body would sink into unconsciousness if the astral body did not illumine it. Likewise the astral body would repeatedly forget the past if the "I" did not rescue this past and carry it over into the present. What death is to the physical body and sleep to the ether body, forgetting is to the astral body. We can also say that life belongs to the etheric body, consciousness to the astral body and memory to the "I"."*

The relationship and functioning of these particular bodies is detailed further by Steiner (1999) in *Body, Soul and Spirit* and Bott (1996) in *Spiritual Science and the Art of Healing*.

Sherwood (2004) reiterates the important connection between the "I" and the breath. Difficult experiences are vibrationally imprinted on the astrality and these experiences result in different combinations of contractions of breath because it is painful to continue breathing into these places of vibrational impact. The contraction in the astrality is carried by the etheric through to the physical body. The "I" presence is carried by the breath so it is extinguished from the parts of the astral, etheric and physical body that become contracted. These are the parts of experience not embraced by the "I". They remain unintegrated in the trauma system which is the repository of such experiences over this life and many lifetimes. These imprints will eventually arise between couples in a relationship.

Energetic languages

The rhythmic, vibrational dynamics of the etheric and astral, create patterns which eventually leave imprints within the cellular structure within the physical body. Consciousness can better access the imprints when equipped with these non-verbal modes of expression, which include sensing, gesturing, visualising, moving and sounding (Sherwood and Tagar 2000).

Sensing is a core language used by lovers and essentially it involves sensing outwards and reading the nonverbal "energies" and the "feelings" of another. It also involves sensing inwards and becoming aware of one's own feelings and energies. Good sensing makes for great love-making and where there is great passion, sensing is usually accurate, unconscious and spontaneous. This, coupled with gesturing and our capacity to read our lover's body language and express through gesture our own feelings, is an essential part of the lover's vocabulary. Creating visual images through visualizing is also a central language in lovers' experiences, as people recreate and create images of their beloved one at will and in many places and times. These visual images fuel the sexual passions and further create bonding between the lovers. Finally, the echoes of the sounds of human vowels and consonants create distinct patterns of energy that resonate within the physical, astral and etheric bodies of the lovers and which connect multiple experiences around the same sound pattern, whether positive or negative (Tagar, 1996). This adds depth to human experience, but also often confuses the immediate present moment experience with reverberating patterns of sound-experiences from other times, other people and other places.

Summary

In the passion of the meeting are the seeds of all that has ever passed between the lovers, but the initial energetic attraction touches the magnificent potential of who they can both be when together which is so much greater and more inspiring than alone. So often lovers comment at the beginning of a relationship; "he is my other half", "together we are greater than alone", "our union blesses other people". Passionate lovers have eyes only for the best in their partner and they hold each other as though beholding a sublime vision of each other's goodness and highest qualities. It is the dream of the best of who we each can be, our golden potential in our best moments. It holds the promise of our deepest yearnings and desires for wholeness.

> *"Love at first sight is always spoken in the past tense. This scene has all the magnificence of an accident: I cannot get over having had this good fortune: to meet what matches my desire"*
>
> *– Barthes, R., A Lover's Discourse: Fragments https://www.goodreads.com/work/quotes/1856185-fragments-d-un-discours-amoureux*

References

Barrett, E. (1850) *Portuguese love sonnets, no 43* https://www.poets.org/poetsorg/poem/how-do-i-love-thee-sonnet-43)

Barthes, R. *A Lover's Discourse: Fragments* https://www.goodreads.com/work/quotes/1856185-fragments-d-un-discours-amoureux (accessed 16-9-16.)

Bott, V. (1995) *Spiritual Science and the Art of Healing,* Healing Arts Press, Vermont.

Bolduc, H. (2016): *Learning from Forty-four Years of Guiding Past-Life Regressions.* http://www.henrybolduc.com/regression.html (accessed 28-9-16)

Fisher, H (2004*) WHY WE LOVE: The Nature and Chemistry of Romantic Love,* Henry Holt, N.Y.

Lawton, I (2008). "The Bloxham Tapes revisited - Why Cryptomnesia is not the Complete Explanation". *Journal of Regression Therapy.* no. 28, vol.1

Fenwick P. Fenwick E (2001*). Past Lives: An Investigation into Reincarnation Memories.* Berkley Books, San Francisco.

Guirdham, A. (1978) *The Cathars and reincarnation.* Watkins, London.

Pert, C (1997) *Molecules of Emotion: the Science behind mind-body medicine.* Touchstone, New York.

Rothschild, B. (2011) *The Body Remembers* Norton and Co., N.Y.

Sachdeva, S. (2012) *The Eight Spiritual Breaths.* Yogi Impressions, Mumbai.

Sherwood, P. and Tagar, Y. (2000) "Experience Awareness tools for preventing Burnout in Nurses". *Australian Journal of Holistic Nursing* April. Vol 7, pp15-20.

Sherwood, P. (2004) *The Healing Art of clay therapy.* Acer, Melboune.

Sherwood, P.(2007) *Holistic counselling: A New Vision for Mental Health.* Sophia publications, Bunbury.

Steiner, R. (1999) reprint. *A Psychology of Body, Soul & Spirit.* Anthroposophic Press, N.Y.

Steiner, R (1994) *Theosophy* Anthroposophic Press, N.Y.

Stundberg, J (2015) *Shotgun awakening: a phenomenological study of the occurrence of extreme experiences of falling in love.* Ph d dissertation, San Francisco, California Institute of Integral Studies San Francisco.

Tagar,Y. (1996) *Philophonetics- Love of sounds: awakening to human experience.* Persephone college publications, Melbourne.

Tennov, D (1979*) Love and Limerence: the experience of being in love.* Stein and Day, N.Y.

Why we Fall in love: www./http://examinedexistence.com/why-we-fall-in-love-the-science-of-love/ (accessed 31-8-16).

Welwood, J. (1985) On love: conditional and unconditional. *Journal of Transpersonal Psychology.* No17, vol.1, pp.33-40.

Woolgar, R. (1988) *Other Lives, Other Selves: A Jungian Psychotherapist Discovers Past Lives.* Doubleday, N.Y.

Woolgar, R. *(2004) Healing Your Past Lives: Exploring the Many Lives of the Soul.* Angus and Robertson, Richmond, B.C.

Woolgar, R. (2006) *Healing you past lives.* Sounds True, Louisville, Co.

CHAPTER 2

The karmas of passion: fusing together

Leighton, Frederic (1856) *The fisherman and the siren*

> When I touched her body,
> I believed she was God.
> In the curves of her form
> I found the birth of Man,
> the creation of the world,
> and the origin of all life.

– Roman Payne www.goodreads.com/quotes/tag/passionate-love

2. The Passion

Sexual connection is oft times elevated to a transcendent realm where the experience of fusion and or dissolution of boundaries with the lover is experienced as sublime. It is an ultimate desire to overcome one's separateness, aloneness and disconnection from the world in which we live, through finding connection. Sexual intimacy is the powerful connection with another person that many people yearn for in the moments of aloneness. This drive to connect is inextricably woven into our hormonal system, and our body and our mind are intertwined drivers in this search for sex, connection and passion.

In the epiphanic moments of sexual intimacy, lovers speak of the dissolution of their boundaries and a fusion into a world of pulsing energy, immersion in a sea of throbbing life without boundaries or forms. Some lovers refer to a range of experiences encapsulated in tantric sex traditions of the East.

> *"The gesture of the amorous embrace seems to fulfil, for a time, the subject's dream of total union with the loved being: The longing for consummation with the other... In this moment, everything is suspended: time, law, prohibition: nothing is exhausted, nothing is wanted: all desires are abolished, for they seem definitively fulfilled... A moment of affirmation; for a certain time, though a finite one, a deranged interval, something has been successful: I have been fulfilled (all my desires abolished by the plenitude of their satisfaction)."*
>
> *Barthes, R., https://www.goodreads.com/work/quotes/1856185-fragments-d-un-discours-amoureux*

Passionate sex can expand our consciousness through such "peak experiences" and then offer us transcendence from our limited, grasping ego. It opens the doorway to the beauty and life of the world. We become more available to life, more

> "The beauty and wisdom of Tantra is that it enhances sexuality as a doorway to the "ecstatic mind of great bliss". Truly, at the peak of orgasm, we pierce through the illusion of fragmentation and separation, and glimpse the unity and interconnectedness of all beings. And through the other–our partner–we fall in love with life."
>
> Anand.,M http://www.lightworkersworld.com/2011/12/tantric-sex-beautiful-quotes-to-trigger-awakening-through-sexuality/

engaged in our world because we are now in love with life. In its best moments, it expands our hearts and minds bringing a new generosity and kindness into our deeds. It leaves us with experiences that we will always remember for in those moments our deepest yearnings as a human being is to reconnect with source: the dynamic patterns of energy that govern our universe and which we have glimpsed. We will always hunger for more so our bonding to our lover intensifies. Sexual union is grasped as a doorway to this ultimate experience and even when sexuality becomes more mundane and less sublime, the passion of the hope of repeating this sublime experience remains. The bonding becomes intense between lovers and frequent and repeated sexual encounters in the relationship, intensify the longing for such sublime encounters. This state of intense longing for sexual fusion with another has variously been described as consummate love, passionate love, extreme love experience, and it often drives the relationship quickly to intimacy and commitment. It is reflected in comments made by a lover when after three days of passionate love with his newfound woman, he says to his parents: "I'm going to marry her".

Astrality or lower mind consciousness

Much has been written about the biochemical foundations and drivers for sexuality, the hormones, but the real glue cannot be understood without reference to the fourfold model outlined previously. In particular, the astral body or lower layers of mind consciousness are dominated by species typical instinctual behaviours such as aggression, dominance, sexuality, and territoriality. The astrality has been described as the reptilian brain (Maclean, 1990). The astral body encapsulates also our parasympathetic and sympathetic nervous system, our "fight or flight" response to stimuli that is automatic, bypassing reflective and insightful intelligence. The astral body is where our fears and desires are recorded energetically as "imprints" or vibrational patterns of experience (Sherwood, 2010, p.25). They are stored in 7-year layers or "sheaths". Many of our defence mechanisms merge out of our struggle to survive and avoid pain on the astral level. These mechanisms result in many aspects of experience being cut off, denied and suppressed. Buried astral experiences often run the life through the unconscious. This trauma/astral system lacks integration with the self system or "I am," and consequently is responsible for many mental health issues. Sardello, cited in Steiner (1999), notes that astrality is engaged in a continuous inner dynamic relationship, between the outer world, mediated by the senses through the physical body, and the intimate realms of inner consciousness.

Nothing in the fourfold model is separate and discrete, all bodies energetically impact upon the others. The astral gives

> "The etheric body is the basis of life, the astral body is the seat of consciousness and consciousness in the physical world is bought at the cost of breaking down or burning physical matter" (Evans and Rodger, 1992, p.39).

shape to the etheric body and weaves a continual dance with the etheric body and its inseparable partner the physical body. The etheric governs the anabolic process in the body, and the astral, the catabolic process in the body. The etheric is governed by the in-breath, the astral by the out-breath and rhythmic balance is essential between the in-breath and out-breath, if physical and emotional health are to be optimised (Sherwood, 2007).

Astral and sexuality

The astral body is also the home of sexuality and this is evidenced by the development of the astral body in adolescence bringing with it sexuality, and intense feelings of anger and anxiety that were less intense and lengthy in childhood. Female astrality incarnates during pre-pubescence and adolescence like a gentle wave, gradually taking the girl out to sea. She begins, often unconsciously by preening herself for prolonged periods particularly focusing upon her hair. For males, the astrality incarnates like an arrow, intense and immediately compelling, as it shoots through the adolescent male's body. It is much stronger than female astrality, so adolescent girls are particularly vulnerable to being flooded by male sexuality, if they engage in early sexual relationships. This often deflects the important task of the girl establishing her own identity or "I". Astrality in adolescent boys is not usually integrated with their "I" and deeper emotional life, and often acts as a separate entity in itself, whereas in adolescent girls, the astrality and sexuality is merged more deeply into their "I". It is clear even in adolescence, that male sexuality is driven primarily by desire while female sexuality is often infused with the ideal of love that she weaves around the man standing beside her. It is not the reality of who he is but the image of whom she desires him to be (Steiner, 2011). Female astrality is infused with the "I" so females experience love and sexuality as intimately linked. Male astrality in contrast, is much more separate from the "I", which is why males often separate out sex from love.

Each time a couple engages in sex, they share in each other's astrality, both its sensuality as well as its stresses. During an orgasm, males download their astral material into their female partner, which relieves them of emotional and mental stressors and often leaves them in a state of sleep, rest or relaxation. They can thus use sex like a "sleeping pill" to release tension in their astral bodies. Females on the other hand, have to process that astral material through their own astral bodies. Women often feel that they "serve" their man through sexuality even when it is driven by their own sexual libido. Initially, this bodily intimacy is characterized by sensuous feelings of delight and joy, passion and pleasure, all parts of the astral system, and so the intimacy increases.

The quality of the astral body is clinging, grasping, cloying and once attached to a sexual object of passion, lovers quickly become enmeshed astrally which is typified by an empty or yearning feeling if separated bodily from their lover, even if they are able to communicate over electronic media. The longing for physical intimacy becomes so great, that often it is the first thing they engage in after a period of physical separation, particularly if it is days or weeks. The astral is the body of desire, which inflames passionate love and provides the fuel for its continuance:

> *"The central fire is desire, and all the powers of our being are given us to see, to fight for, and to win the object of our desire. Quench that fire and man turns to ashes."*
> Materin, B., http://www.notable-quotes.com/d/desire_quotes.html

Astrality and limerence

The characteristics of the astral body that enmesh lovers are reflected in the characteristics of limerence, which has been defined as:

> *"an involuntary interpersonal state that involves intrusive, obsessive, and compulsive thoughts, feelings and behaviours that are contingent on perceived emotional reciprocation from the object of interest"*
> (Watkin and Vo, 2008, p. 15)

The astrality is compulsively driven, often by intense and irrational feelings that may be aversions or desires. Its cloying qualities mean that once attached to an object or person of desire, it is difficult to extricate oneself or to exist sufficiently independently, to view the situation with some insight. The astral body is also characterized by extremes in feelings: the lover is either in great jubilation or deep despair, particularly if separation from the loved one is occurring either through distance or lack of reciprocity. Core to the limerent experience and the astral body, is the tendency to idealize that which is desired in the present moment and to ignore that which is undesirable. This selective perception produces a romanticised view of the lover that is not grounded in the realities of character and behaviours.

Passionate love and the fourfold model

Given the power and intensity of the astral body when sexuality is unleashed, sexuality will take control of the etheric flows and through the etheric, the physical body. The intensity of astrality varies with different individuals and it is reflected in the intensity of a person's drives, including their sex drives. Those persons with high sex drives will have intense astral bodies. The counter-balancing body is the 'I', the higher mind consciousness, that is capable of insight, critical reflection, strategic depth in thinking, inspiration and higher order faculties. It is the "I" that provides the moral centre for a person to evaluate the skilfulness or otherwise of a passionate sexual encounter or relationship. The "I" should always chaperone the astral, which should not be allowed out without this skilful companion.

One needs to understand that it is the "I" to "I" recognition in the first meetings that draws couples together to form intimate relationships together with the astral "sympatico". One cannot be sexually attracted to someone with whom one has not had many sexual encounters in the past. The intensity of the passion of the attraction is connected to the depth and breadth of the past meetings in other lives. The greater the attraction and passion, the greater the shared encounters with each other in the past. At the beginning of passionate love, it is the mutual delight in each other, the sharing of realities not previously shared with others, and the acceptance of each other into an intimate bodily space, that bonds the relationship and cements it towards commitment.

How these different aspects of our human constitution come together in intimate relationships will be illustrated throughout this book, using a number of composite case-studies. These case studies will be used to track the development of a passionate love relationship and illustrate what goes right and what goes wrong at the deepest karmic levels. These case studies are derived from a number of encounters with clients working with passionate lover relationships and represent no one couple but rather, core themes in these types of relationships. They also represent passionate lover relationship at three different phases of the adult life : the twenties, the thirties and the forties.

Illustrative case studies: the karmic meeting

Rachel and Ben

Rachel, a nurse in her late forties, ten years after her divorce met Bruce an engineer and recently divorced. Although they had four children between them, they were all young adults and lived away from home. Rachel had migrated from England to Australia as a child and Ben was Australian born. They were both financially secure and their first meeting was classic of passionate lovers. What was a short morning coffee together turned into eight hours of conversation, lunch, dinner, chocolates and sex. They moved at an astonishingly fast speed headlong into an intimate relationship and within a couple of months, Rachel was a permanent resident at Ben's house. At different times, during the first year of the relationship, they both spoke of "how right they were for each other," how well matched they were physically, intellectually and in terms of common interests and perspectives on the world". They both bemoaned time apart and had a passionate sexual life on a daily basis. Both believed that they were made for each other. They praised each other's talents, celebrated each other's successes at work and supported each other through the challenges that came their way. The despair that had marred Ben's life prior to meeting Rachel, disappeared and he found new purpose, motivation and rhythm in his life. She supported him emotionally through his dark times and regrets and grief over his failed marriage and lost job opportunities. She, who had raised her children alone, found his support on a myriad of practical issues in life of inestimable value. They had everything going for them and ticked all the boxes of successful relationship indicators. They were a complementary team. She jollied him out of his melancholia and he inspired her with his amazing conversations and knowledge. They shared many common interests, were never short of an engaging conversation on politics, ethics, life or philosophy. On all levels, they were well suited. They were both intelligent well-educated people and this seemed a meeting and a "match made in heaven". The "I" to "I" meeting was strong as they recognised each other's potential and the potential they could have as a working couple together in a joint business adventure. Their astral passion and sexual intimacy, was intense and enmeshing on a daily basis. They became engaged twelve months into the relationship, with plans to marry at two years.

Kate and Ian

Kate, a beautician and Ian, a chiropractor both in their mid-thirties and not yet having found their "life-partner" met when her vehicle was broken down at the side of a isolated country road and he had stopped to see if she needed help. It was only after several dates that they decided that they were destined for each other and in love. Both had come from homes where their parents had gone through bitter divorces so they were cautious in their commitments and the speed at which they moved into the relationship. Nevertheless within six months, they were clearly an "item" among their friends and had plans to move in together at twelve months. They had so many interests in common, a love of nature, interest in travel and boating. They complimented each other well. Kate's sensitive introverted nature was balanced by Ian's more extroverted jovial nature and she experienced feeling secure and protected in her presence. He enjoyed her gentleness, and was besotted by her beauty, voice and stylish dress. At last, they believed that they had found their soul-mate and decided to begin purchasing a house together. Their wedding which was planned to be in Bali, in a year's time.

Fiona and Michael

Fiona, a teacher, was 26 years of age when she fell in love with Michael whom she had met at a friend's party. He was 28, still searching for his career while working in a Telco. They had no children, no properties and both lived in rentals, Fiona in a share house of six, and Michael with two of his mates. They both had a passion for sport and keeping fit, so they spent hours together keeping fit at the gym. They both believed that they were destined for each other and after six months moved in together in their own couple rental. They planned to live together for a couple of years before marriage and children. Each stated that the first 6 months living together was "wonderful", their sex and social life was amazing and both appreciated and valued each other's strengths and gifts. Fiona particularly admired Michael's sports reputation and he valued her role as a sport's teacher. They were deeply in love and became engaged within two years.

Summary

The all-consuming passion of lovers is fuelled by the astral body, which is the home of the sensory life mediated out to the world through the body. The astral body is carrying our sexuality, desires and passions to create an intense energetic bond with our loved one. Through sexual intimacy the astralities of the two persons bond together and all that is contained therein is shared and aroused. In that sense, astral passion is addictive ever driving lovers to more and more, its desires never entirely satisfied. Unless chaperoned by the "I", the astral passion initially drives blindly through the relationship, seeing only the positive and ignoring and downplaying any warning signs that all may not be well. The astral body drives the passion through the physical and etheric bodies creating a longing, yearning and desire for continued connectedness with the loved one. It is without logic or insight. For many, it is the sole destination in the relationship.

> *"Love is passion. Obsession. Someone you cannot live without. Someone you fall head over heels for. Find someone you love like crazy, and will love you the same back...to make the journey without falling deeply in love; you have not lived life at all..."*
>
> Black., J *https://www.google.com.au/search?q=quotes+love+and+passion*

References

Anand, M. http://www.lightworkersworld.com/2011/12/tantric-sex-beautiful-quotes-to-trigger-awakening-through-sexuality/ (accessed 1-9-16).

Black, J. *https://www.google.com.au/search?q=quotes+love+and+passion* (accessed 30-8-16).

Barthes,R. *A Lover's Discourse: Fragments* https://www.goodreads.com/work/quotes/1856185-fragments-d-un-discours-amoureux (accessed 1/9/16.)

Evans, M. and Rodger, I. (1992) *Complete Healing: regaining your health through Anthroposophical medicine.* Anthroposophical Press, N.Y.

MacLean, Paul D. (1990). *The triune brain in evolution: role in paleocerebral functions.* Plenum Press, N.Y.

Materin, B.*, http://www.notable-quotes.com/d/desire_quotes.html (*accessed 10-9-16).

Sherwood, P (2010) *Holistic counselling: a new vision for Mental Health.* Sophia Publications, Bunbury.

Sherwood, P (2007) *Infertility to fertility.* Sophia Publications, Bunbury.

Steiner, R. (2011*) Sexuality, Love and Partnership.* Rudolf Steiner Press, N.Y.

Steiner, R. (1999) *A Psychology of Body, Soul and Spirit.* Steiner Press, N.Y.

Wakin,A & Vo, B. (2008) *Love Variant: The wakin-vo I.D.R. model of limerence.* http//www.interdisciplinary.net/ptb/persons/pil/pil2wakinvo%20paper.pdf.

Chapter 3
Karmic differences: challenges to intimacy

Burne-Jones, Edward (1888) *The doom fulfilled*

" The meeting between two personalities is like the contact of two chemical substances: if there is any reaction both are transformed."

– CG Jung http://www.trans4mind.com/quotes/quotes-communication-relationships.html

Dr Patricia Sherwood

3. Complementarity to difference

The binding and blinding passion of the early lover relationship with its focus on union, similarity and complementarity increasingly gives way to a growing awareness of differences. Human beings have not been very good at managing differences and intimate relationships are a particularly intense arena for their manifestation. The physical differences between a man and a woman are obvious. She nurtures new life; he is the one who stands in the world as her protector and the protector of the children they have co-created. She connects most strongly to community and interpersonal relationships; he to the world in an objectified way where conquest of tasks and objects is his primary focus. Her body is flowing, soft in its curves and her brain has larger areas for interpersonal survival like communication and emotions. His body is more angular and stands more strongly upon the earth and generally, his physical strength far exceeds hers. These differences are generalisations but readily observable in many couples. Differences that have been empirically observed include brain functioning and structure. Male brains utilize

> *"Though no one notices at the time, in-loveness obliterates the humanity of the beloved. One does a curious kind of insult to another by falling in love with him, for we are really looking at our own projection of God, not at the other person. If two people are in love, they tread on stardust for a time and live happily ever after—that is so long as this experience of divinity has obliterated time for them. Only when they come down to earth do they have to look at each other realistically and only then does the possibility of mature love exist."*
>
> (Johnson, *1991*)

seven times more grey matter than female brains and grey matter produces focused, localised, single task skill sets. Females on the other hand have ten times more white matter which embraces the networking grid of the brain, facilitating multi-tasking and quick transitions from one task to another (Jantz, G., 2014). Male brains also have to process more testosterone. This tends to produce aggression and drive more physical activity, while female brain chemistry has more oxytocin, a chemical that promotes bonding and social interactions. Another significant difference is that females generally have a larger memory centre and consequently access and retain emotional and sensory input at higher levels than males. They are often much more articulate and have verbal centres on both sides of the brain, while men have verbal centres only on the left side of the brain. One of the most common gender differences to emerge in therapy is that females articulate and recount hurtful things that they recall were said by their partners, while their male partners often do not even recall the event. Jantz (2014) describes why this occurs:

> *"The female brain, in part thanks to far more natural blood flow throughout the brain at any given moment (more white matter processing), and because of a higher degree of blood flow in a concentration part of the brain called the cingulate gyrus, will often ruminate on and revisit emotional memories more than the male brain. Males tend, after reflecting more briefly on an emotive memory, to analyse it somewhat, and then move onto the next task. During this process, they may also choose to change course and do something active and unrelated to feelings rather than analyse their feelings at all."*

Women generally feel more deeply and with more complexly

than males, who divert feelings into thinking and actions in the world, and in this difference lies the potential for a world of misunderstanding. So many women in therapy wail about not being understood by their partners or being deeply hurt by comments he has made to them, but now he does not even recall the event. To add to the wound, women often complain that he wants to mend differences through sex, but she needs to talk about the problem until a new understanding is reached. Males often complain that they show their love by doing things for her and working hard, and in exchange, they want sex and appreciation. Much has been written about these differences and John Gray's (1992) *Men are from Mars and Women are from Venus* became a landmark book in this field:

> *"When a man can listen to a woman's feelings without getting angry and frustrated, he gives her a wonderful gift. He makes it safe for her to express herself. The more she is able to express herself, the more she feels heard and understood, and the more she is able to give a man the loving trust, acceptance, appreciation, admiration, approval, and encouragement that he needs."*

However, these levels of interaction derived from different biological factors on the physical level and from different brain chemistry are of course generalisations because there is a huge range of differences even within the same genders. However, differences dominate the relationship as it matures over time and not only differences at the observable biological levels but also, in relation to the more subtle bodies that are not directly observable, namely, the etheric and the astral.

Etheric

The etheric body has a profound influence on the flow of emotional life through the physical body as it reflects energetic experience from the sensory world, via the astral, into the physical body. The etheric body is female in males and male in females (Steiner, 2011). Thus, while males are physically more robust, they are emotionally more vulnerable. Females being emotionally masculine are emotionally more resilient than males. Steiner (1980) enlarges his concept thus:

> *"a man becomes a warrior through the outer courage of his bodily nature, a woman possesses an inner courage, the courage of sacrifice and devotion. The man brings his creative activity to bear on external life. The woman works with devoted receptivity into the world... In the man, the masculine pole works outwards and the feminine lives more inwardly, while in the woman the opposite is true."*

Essentially a woman manifests her feminine qualities in the world and her masculine qualities in her inner life which makes her more robust than a man when dealing with inner emotional trauma. He is more robust than her when dealing with physical circumstances in the world. He is emotionally very vulnerable. Nowhere is this difference as obvious as when relationships break up. The man is emotionally devastated and as the etheric of the woman is withdrawn from him, he speaks of feeling "gutted" and emptied out. The woman, on the other hand, senses etherically the withdrawal of the man's etheric as exposing her in the world. She feels vulnerable in the world. Here we see at the emotional level, the reverse of the experience at the physical level during intercourse. It is not surprising then, that women do better emotionally outside of relationship, while men do better emotionally inside relationship. The quality of the feminine and masculine in each gender reflects the cumulative experiences of many lifetimes. All people have experiences in both genders. These complex past experiences do profoundly affect how they incarnate into the particular biological gender in this present life. (Steiner, R 1980).

"I am"

Psychologically, from a Jungian perspective, the male/female differences are profound. While Jung does not speak of the physical body as feminine in a woman and her etheric as masculine and vice-versa in a man, he still identifies these dualities of female/male within each gender. He notes that the obvious gender of the physical body, prevents most people from realising that they have the qualities of the opposite gender in their unconscious and that this male/female duality within each person must be addressed for their own psychological health. It is the primary task of the female to come to terms with the often unconscious masculine within herself, her "animus", and for a male to come to terms with his often unconscious female within him, his anima. This struggle, if ignored, as an inner dynamic within one's psyche, will result in being projected onto one's partner and cause considerable disquiet in a relationship (Jung, 1964). If it is entirely repressed then it may result in serious depression, where a person feels unable to flourish in their life. In traditional patriarchical society, a man prefers a woman to remain unconscious and be only in touch with her compliant feminine. He feels that if she would agree to do things his way, there will be peace in the household. He decides important issues and he must take control and she must acquiesce. Now women are increasingly financially independent, cultural values have changed, and for independent women, such a model of relationships is anaethema. They are in touch with their "animus" or masculine side as they now work in the world and have to come to terms with the demands of a masculine oriented workplace. They have their own income in many cases, and they thus have the financial power to direct their own growth and lives. Agreeing with their partner, even for peace, wears very thin, especially after the children have grown up and/or when they earn similar or larger incomes. Increasingly, more and more women will no longer wait for this time, but stand up for their different ideas early in the relationship. Therefore, negotiation and communication are becoming increasingly central demands in human relationships. Sexual passion alone cannot overcome differences between partners in relationships.

A man is generally very unconscious of his own anima, of his own internal feeling life and projects it onto the woman to bear it for him. The beautiful, white clad bride is the perfect "anima" image for the victorious man who feels that this icon of feminine beauty and peace shall carry his emotional life and fulfil his relationship dreams. While initially she may often idolise him as her hero, her protector, the man of her dreams, being wed and child bearing for a woman is also a death experience.

It is the ending of a life of freedom and the beginning of a life of sacrifice and responsibility for new life and her husband (Johnson, R., 1989). It is common for a woman to present in therapy feeling trapped and exhausted by her relationship and resentful that he is so unavailable to help when she most needs it. He topples from her tower of adoration and she sees his feet of clay. Her resentment and anger can bewilder a man who sees himself as working hard in the world to provide for his family and children. He oft times feels when this occurs, that he has fallen from her grace, which is a cold and fearful experience for a man. He now feels rejected from his paradise, or at least, no longer the king of his own castle.

Astrality

As mentioned previously, the astral body contains all the imprints of previous experiences stored like dirty dishes one upon the other in energetic patterns of resonance. Through sexual intercourse, not only do the etheric bodies of the man and woman start to meld and create a single etheric body over the period of two years, but also their astral bodies interplay energetically very intimately. They become able to access wounded parts of their lover without even trying and energetically these come to the surface. Many lovers report having experienced tears during sex. This may be because of the tender beauty and joy of the process, which is healing hurt and sorrow around previous scarred sexual relationships which are now resurfacing during a similar trigger experience, or because they suddenly feel extraordinarily vulnerable, often not even in a conscious way. The astral body carries within it the element of fire that is easily aroused into a conflagration in challenging circumstances in which it feels threatened. Governed by the primitive flight or fight instinct, the astral body either fights back in moments of fear, or, disappears and retreats from the relationship. Which response, depends on the level of fear, previous karmas between the lovers and, of course, early attachment patterns with the primary caregiver, usually the mother. The astral body or lower mind acts in these ways in relationships when we act instinctively, without the conscious insertion of our "I" or spirit into the astral experience. It is the "I" that must penetrate the astrality, if relationships are to flourish. Otherwise, the astrality when triggered by fear or anger becomes a wild beast, rampaging against others or itself. The astrality needs an insightful driver, and this can only be our "I".

These reactive elements of the astral are easily triggered between lovers by a myriad of minor day to day comments or interactions. Criticism and judgment of the other's actions provide a major trigger for astral flare-ups. In addition, differences of opinion, different approaches to child raising, different social and personal values and power struggles over decision making are other major trigger points. The astral body is very sticky and can be imaged as a spider wanting to spin its sticky webs around those around it and entrap others in its own agendas, no matter how one sided and warped they may be. As long as one of the lovers resists the bait and remains calm and collected, and holds the middle space, all is well. An argument arising from the astral, the home of fear, anger and anxiety, will eventually calm down for lack of fuel if one party refuses to engage in the turmoil. The lover's temptation when touched by sticky webs of astrality is to recoil or fight back and enter the fray with the initial intention to defend themself from the accusation or criticisms. This is fatal and will end in embroiling both persons in reaction to reaction which results in senseless, useless arguing, futile outbursts of anger, with neither party in a position to act or speak skilfully. It is really like shooting on friendly forces, a dangerous and ultimately deadly strategy in an intimate relationship. When the astral is reactive, there is no insight, memory, learning or skilful conflict resolution. These are all qualities of the presence of the higher mind or the "I". One can guarantee that a person is stuck in the astral when they display a cluster of the following characteristics:

rapid talking and over-talking with lots of repetition

intellectualizing or rationalizing to avoid feelings

rapid breathing

glazed eyes

memory loss over flaring up

certainty that they are right

telling the other person what the other person thinks and feels

blaming and "you-ing" the other person

not using the word "I" to own their thoughts, feelings and reactions calling the other person insulting names

blaming the other person for making them feel, angry, bad, fearful or anything else adverse.

Sherwood (2010, p.190) details the characteristics between reactive unskilful states and speaking or skilful "I" states as detailed in the table below:

Table 1: Reaction versus speaking

Reaction	Speaking
Constricted breathing: feel tension in the body	Flowing breathing: do not feel tension in the body
Not Owning experience "you make me"	Owning experience " I feel"
"Astral" origin	"I " origin
Excarnating: "I" leaves	Incarnating: "I" is present
Repetitive statements	Clear incisive statements
Dull glazed look in eyes	Bright, alert present look
"I" is not present	"I" is present
Intellectualising: dead feeling	Speaking clear feelings
Judgments of others	Non-judgmental
Often seeing the trigger person or event as all bad / evil and that we feel better if they stop the provoking behaviour	Perceiving the trigger person or event as a messenger of our own inner states of discord that require healing
Anger or fear or hysterical grief	Centred stillness in feeling life
Listeners are often bored or discount the response as irrational	Listeners are alert and sense the truth speaking
Response out of proportion to the trigger event	Response in proportion to the trigger event
Triangulate other parties into alliances against the trigger person.	Speak directly to the person involved.

Unfortunately, when both lovers are speaking from the reactive, astral position there is little hope for the relationship. At this time, both lovers are not their adult ages, but have regressed into child like wounded places, although externally they appear to be adults. To illustrate, I will use a case study example. Ben criticises Rachel for the meal she has cooked. It is just not good enough or in some way not to his liking. Rachel reacts angrily and tells Ben he can cook his own meals in future and Ben reacts by retreating into his shell and sulking claiming that Rachel does not love him. An argument ensures and Rachel regresses to her 5 years old being criticised by her demanding mother who was never happy with the tasks Rachel completed around the home. They were "never good enough". Ben has become his 6 year old who has been rejected by his father after requesting that they play football in a different way that is easier for Ben. Neither lover is conscious of the real wounded dynamics at play and continue to focus on the immediately presenting trigger: the meal issue. The real issue is Rachel's hurt from her childhood of criticism and Ben's woundedness at his father's constant rejection. Such lover interactions are not uncommon and are very damaging to the etheric sheaths of both parties, particularly causing wounding to the heart sheath that is initially, open between lovers when the relationship begins in a loving manner. With repeated assaults, the heart closes its sheath for its own protection, and in the process, much of the joy between the lovers starts to dry up. Sexuality is also affected, becoming less delightful and more perfunctory.

In addition, the sexual hormones that charge the relationship with extra energy and zap, start to decline after 6 months, again at 12 months, and finally, after two years, tend to establish themselves at a baseline. This means that sexual passion alone will not hold together the widening cracks in a faltering relationship. The relationship is now reaching a critical stage where the lovers will either "make it or break it". Their actions in relation to emerging differences are critical. The antidote to this astral chaos and pain lies in the 'I" or the higher consciousness which is characterised by skilful thought, insight and self-reflective capacities.

"I" and making the relationship flourish

"I" in intimate relationships: differentiation and individualization

Schnarch (1997) skilfully points out that differentiation among mature adults in intimate relationships is a critical quality wherein each person balances their individuality with the emotional connection. The core human need is for ongoing growth of the "I" in each partner so that they can more wholly manifest their unique gifts and qualities. This can be seriously curtailed in an intimate relationship because of "fusion fantasies". These can be defined as the belief that there is only one position and one view possible and that this is desirable in the couple relationships. Differences are to be avoided. In addition, one or both of the lovers equate agreement with being loved and accepted. Differences and disagreements will then lead to estrangement and a concerted campaign to eliminate different opinions by controlling the other person through money or emotional pressure, so that they conform to the accepted world view of the dominant person.

The irony is that through enforcing conformity around issues in relationship, conflict or mental health breakdown then become the arena for asserting unique identity. Each person tries to distance themselves from the other through unproductive conflict, in order to retain some sense of identity. This has very unhealthy impacts on intimacy and sexuality. Partners prone to maintaining the "fusion fantasy", often, in Schnarch's view, have had an over-controlling parent and love was dependent upon compliance with that parent's values and world views. The healthy model is differentiation, where each person in the relationship has the freedom and respect from the other person to develop their own unique style, opinions, and activities and still remain lovingly accepted by the other person. There is then room in this relationship for ongoing growth for both individuals, as well as between the couple. Underlying healthy differentiation is a valuing of difference.

Appreciation of difference

The "I" in relationship is the driver of positive conflict resolution and appreciation of difference. The single greatest factor in maintaining the passion and love in intimate relationships is understanding and appreciation of the different gifts that each person brings to the relationship, rather than criticising their differences. As Gray (1992) notes: "when men and women are

Lover relationships and karma

able to respect and appreciate their differences, their love has a chance to blossom." Essentially, it requires the discipline of seeing the best in each other and focusing and celebrating each other's strengths. Differences because of gender or character can be perceived as complementary and powerful. Bougeret beautifully describes her experience of the complementarity of gender differences :

> *"A woman in love respects and raises up her man. She is his constant source of support. She matches his heart and passions with her own. She sees the very best in him, even when he does not. She is his foundation; what he returns home to.*
>
> *A man in love is cautious with the decisions he makes, words he says and actions he takes, so he never purposefully causes her pain. He believes in her when she struggles believing in herself. He is her foundation, where she feels safe to be her true self."*
>
> Bourgeret http://www.goodreads.com/quotes/tag/passionate-love

Core to appreciating and celebrating differences in lover relationships, is the regular and mutual expression of gratitude (McCraty,R. and Childre, D., 2004.) Finding something daily to praise about the other person and telling them is crucial. Research has found that gratitude is the single most important emotion in the health of the heart. Without a healthy heart, relationships will eventually succumb to disease. In therapy, I frequently give couples in trouble, the exercise of daily, for 30 days, writing a note to each other expressing one thing about the presence of their partner in their life for which they are grateful. Couples unable to do this are in bad shape and the long term prognosis for the relationship is not good.

Communicating from the "I"

Healthy communication between couples starts with couples understanding and acting upon the statement that: "You can tell me what you think and feel but you cannot tell me what I think and feel". Essentially, this is another way of saying that each person in the relationship must own their own thoughts and feelings and speak from the "I" position. So for example, instead of "you make me feel angry when you don't give the children dinner at the correct time" rephrase the statement to "I feel angry when I notice that the children have not had dinner at the agreed upon time". This requires each person in the relationship to recognise and accept that they are responsible for their own thoughts and feelings and cannot blame the other person for how they think and feel. In the case of the children's dinnertime, they need to deal with their own feelings of anger and not project them onto their partner. They can then have a skilful conversation from an "I" position rather than the angry reactive astral position about why they feel it is important for the children to eat at that particular time. They may be able get their partner to agree that this is a good idea and then the matter is easily resolved. Their partner, however, may not be invested in when the children eat so is unwilling to commit to a particular time. This then gives the other person the option of ensuring that the children eat at a set time when they are around by preparing the food for them, or letting the matter go entirely. This confronts one with differences in child rearing practices. The couple have to decide in the overall relationship, how important is this issue and how can it be best resolved by both parties working from a skilful, insightful position.

Refraining from reacting: speaking instead from the "I" position.

Refraining from reactive behaviour, the fight response "anger," or the flight response "fear," are very difficult challenges in all relationships because the presenting triggers in relationship, fear or anger, are actually "stirring" up imprints in the astral body from an earlier experience of trauma, or in some cases, several earlier experiences of trauma. In its simplest form, this trauma comes from early childhood woundings usually under the age of 14 years, during which the child had few defences against the external environment. Traumatic imprints of experience may transcend this event in childhood and flow into past lives or DNA memories and these profoundly affect the present moment because they resonate with the same pattern. So for example, when Rachel reacts because she feels judged by Ben, then this triggers the wounded childhood relationship with her critical mother. However, underlying that, may be life-times of experience of being judged by partners or communities as being inadequate. If any of those judgments were associated with painful trials and deaths, then Rachel's level of fear or anger will be significantly disproportionate to the triggers in her current relationship. The bodily cell memory that stores all experiences through the astrality does not make any time differentiation between the same energetic experiences. In the body's energetic experience, they are all concurrent in the present moment (Hawkins, 1995).

At this level of reactiveness, counselling and therapy is recommended to transform and heal these energetic patterns so that they no longer contaminate the present relationship. If the reactiveness is less serious, then simple anger management techniques can be useful. These focus upon restoring the contracted breathing in the body caused by the anger through aerobic exercises or other activities. It is important to note that sulkiness, moodiness, sarcasm and bitchiness are secondary manifestations of anger that is imploded rather than exploded, but have the same origins and need to be addressed.

The astral body and karmic patterns

In addition to astral material that emerges from unresolved childhood experiences that are triggered by adults caught in their fear and unmet needs, their aversions and desires, there is also underpinning karmic material from previous lives, which exacerbates the problems between couples. The unconsciousness of couples in relation to these patterns and imprints behind the immediately presenting issues, explains why on quiet reflection and in moments of insight, couples often wonder why they had such intense reactions to such trivial incidents. The presenting issue in the present moment, is the trigger to a particular vibrational pattern stored in the layers of the astral body, which is brought to the surface by the resonance it has with the presenting trigger issues. In other words, they are stored on a similar vibrational pattern and when the chord is struck in the present life, it reverberates through the astral body and all experiences around that chord/tone resonate within the physical body.

This unconsciousness is the cause of much unresolved angst in intimate relationships and the greater the initial passion and attraction between a couple, the greater the amount of such long term karmic resonances there are between the couple.

To illustrate, Kate and Ian presented in counselling because she was feeling very suppressed and trapped by Ian's reaction to her speaking or laughing loudly in their home. Although they lived on a spacious suburban block, Ian was always fearful that the neighbours might hear them talking even inside the house. His imploded anger was particularly evident if she tried to discuss a matter on which they disagreed and whenever possible he shut down the conversation. Kate being very vibrant and energetic felt that this was undermining the quality of their communication and her sense of security in the relationship was diminished. The underlying astral issue in this life triggered by Ian repressing loud conversation in the home was his fear of public humiliation. He had been mortified as an adolescent when his mother used to stand on the balcony of their two storey house and scream out obscenities about his father. Kate's fear of suppression tracked back to her first relationship as teenager that was marred by domestic violence. Her partner did not permit her to talk to anyone but himself, even when they went out and she had no phone access or access to postal services. They lived in an isolated farmhouse where she was regularly physically abused. Here, we can note, that the presenting relationship between Kate and Ian is not marred by domestic violence or verbal abuse. Rather, the problem is the resonance of a small part of their existing interaction around communication in the house with traumatic unresolved experiences from their earlier relationships in this life. The body cannot distinguish linear time. In the body all experience is concurrent in the present moment even experiences coming from past lives/DNA cellular material. As we penetrated more deeply into this issue with Kate and Ian the following emerged. Kate went back to a previous life in which she had been a servant in a wealthy household and she had been blamed for stealing some precious china or family heirloom. She tried to protest her innocence but was not allowed to speak up by the person in charge of the household servants. That person had energetic similarities to Ian. In that life, he organised her dismissal and she eventually died of starvation on the streets. This incident helps to explain the intensity of Kate's fear around feeling she cannot speak up in the present scenario, even though the present relationship with Ian, is not threatening. There is sufficient resonance or similarity for her body to be triggered into intense fear. Ian on the other hand, when in counselling, recalled a life in which he had been betrayed by his wife who had spread lies around the neighbourhood about his behaviour that led him to be ostracized by the community and he was dismissed from his high status position in the government of his day. Again, this intense past life experience resounds within Ian's physical body because of the trigger of similarity with the current day presenting issue. In his bodily experience, all experiences are concurrent in the present moment.

The astral body stores its material from the present to the past, and it takes a particular act of mind consciousness and training to be able to insert one's "I" into the astral body and uncover the underlying astral pattern in earlier experiences in this life, and in previous experiences in other lives. This, however, is vitally necessary to reveal the hidden intense dynamics that are running the current reactions of fear. Once these experiences are uncovered, then interventions can be made to release these stuck energetic patterns for both parties, so the breath, can flow clearly and freely again within each person and between the couples. The precise interventions required to achieve these healing transformations are documented in Sherwood (2010, p.245).

"I" and breaking the relationship

In their book *Quest of the Mythical Mate,* Bader and Pearson (1988) also highlight the profound implications of the resolution of the individuality versus mutuality paradox. Differentiation is in their view, the key to satisfactory couple development. They name the sequential stages of each relational development: symbiosis, differentiation, practice, rapprochement, and mutual interdependence. However, if only one individual chooses to continue to grow and develop and the other individual clings onto a more primitive level of differentiation that they manifest through their "fusion fantasies" then, inevitably the gap between both partners will become too wide, the conflict too endemic and the relationship will break up. Each person will then gravitate towards some new partner who will more likely be closer to their level of differentiation or "I" development.

Unresolved blame and criticism

The astral system because of its fears and aversions, and its unmet desires and needs is prone to direct their needs and demands towards another person. If feeling upset or unhappy, then blame and criticism directed at the partner are often the result. The other person is blamed for their unhappiness by this primitive form of consciousness that drives the astral body. Many unaware couples take it for granted that their partners are responsible for their happiness. This is an approach fraught with danger and it ignores the blatant fact that we are in control of our own thoughts and feelings and, we can choose to be happy, angry, sad or otherwise. It is this failure to take responsibility for ourselves, that ultimately leads to unhealthy co-dependence or the break-up of the relationship.

The uncontrolled astral body with its imploded and exploded anger, rage, moodiness, blame and criticism is a fearful creature with which to live in relationships. When both parties are afflicted by such a rampantly uncontrolled part of themselves, then the relationship will be in deep trouble and eventually a break up or break down is inevitable. One partner will leave voluntarily or one partner may develop an illness like depression, which effectively marginalises them in the relationship. It is essential that the reactive astral body be named and tamed in the couple relationship if the relationship is to experience longevity.

Couple case studies

Rachel and Ben

Rachel and Ben's relationship occurring in the mid-life stage, was already characterized by considerable differentiation. Both had their own careers, their own home, their children and their own interests and life styles. Ben who came from a family in which the mother was very controlling and there was only one world view allowed, hers, was already well socialised into the "fusion fantasy". He believed that love came from compliance. Rachel, on the other hand, had been her own boss for a decade and had developed her own successful career and lifestyle. Conflict was inevitable as both persons were intelligent and self-opinionated persons. Ben felt hurt if she did not support his position with his adult children on a particular issue, while she insisted she could not pretend to support something that she did not agree with or did not find skilful. He was challenged that she was not interested in combining their joint assets or properties but felt they should instead establish something new co-jointly themselves now. The list of differences although considerable was initially masked by the satisfying sex, and many shared activities around travel, art, culture and history. He was intelligent and she loved his mind as much as his body. He definitely preferred her body but was flattered to be with a woman of intellect and passion.

The biggest trigger in their astral connection was criticism. She was quite capable of criticising his neglect of the environment in his lifestyle that included everything from the dishwashing liquid, to mountains of plastic bags, to the washing powder and cleaning substances in his house. Living primarily in his house, she was more vulnerable to his daily criticisms over how she washed the dishes, cooked the food, cleaned the house, washed the clothes, and watered the garden. At times, she cried, at other times she was angry but mostly she remembered not to react. Rachel had completed personal development courses, so tried to speak from the "I" position and to avoid unnecessary arguments by silently appreciating his experience, but knowing hers was different. Ben believed strongly that a particular view was either right or wrong. It was inevitable that he was high on "fusion fantasy" and the relationship tended to be dominated from time to time, with prolonged arguments in which Ben was certain that he was right and with frustration that Rachel refused to agree with his viewpoint.

Kate and Ian

Kate and Ian had most conflicts over differences around child raising. While they were more able to allow each other the space to have very different opinions and experiences individually, when it came to raising the children, Kate wanted it her way most of the time and Ian felt marginalised. She told him how to do everything in relation to the children, what they were to wear, what they were to eat and when they were to sleep or play. Kate and Ian both worked part time and one day when Kate returned from work, she became very angry with Ian when she noticed that he had not cooked dinner nor cleaned the house that day as was on the agreed roster. Her criticism triggered Ian into an angry outburst about being controlled by Kate and he stormed out of the house and smashed a garden ornament. He felt unappreciated and Kate experienced being abandoned and uncared about. In therapy, the major childhood issues underlying this incident were Kate's experience of her father smashing a wedding photo before leaving the family home for three years. Ian's trauma came from witnessing his mother verbally attacking and criticising his father throughout his childhood for not being a good enough provider. Working on these astral experiences resulted in far fewer angry outbursts on Kate's part around issues of Ian's childcare, and Ian became more resilient to the fewer criticisms that did occur that were directed at his child-care efforts.

Fiona and Michael

Neither Fiona or Michael had "fusion fantasies". They were both happy to have different opinions and to engage in different activities. Fiona enjoyed activities with her female friends, Michael with his mates. They had both come from securely attached childhood experiences and consequently found it relatively easy not to need to conform to the other person's expectation in order to be loved and to feel positive about themselves. They enjoyed sports together around which they could be competitive but content.

Summary

The challenge in this phase of relationship is to negotiate a skilful pathway between differentiation and sameness, between individualisation and intimacy. It is a strange paradox, but we best achieve healthy intimacy by individuation, that is by both persons becoming the unique and wonderful persons that they are and celebrating and valuing each other's differences. The astral body which is so triggered by differences particularly by criticism and perceived failure to meet its needs can only be successfully tamed in relationships by a strong individuated "I". If not the astral body of both parties eventually becomes like a wild fire, scorching even the best of what the couple have to offer each other. It is essential that to tame the astral body, one needs to energetically transform the past energetic imprints from childhood and maybe past lives if the problem is persistent. Just dealing with the presenting issue is insufficient. Then, only can couples develop sufficient insight into the dynamics of relationships and take responsibility for the aversions and desires that characterise their astrality. Then, they create the freedom in a relationship to be intimate, passionate and unique.

> *"If we are courageous enough to say, "Not this person, nor any other, can ultimately give me what I want; only I can," then we are free to celebrate a relationship for what it can give."*
> James Hollis, *Eden project*
> http://www.goodreads.com/quotes/tag/individuation

References

Bourgeret, E. http://www.goodreads.com/quotes/tag/passionate-love (accessed 1-9-16).

Bader, E., & Pearson, P.T. (1988). *In quest of the mythical mate: A developmental approach to diagnosis and treatment in couples therapy.* Brunner/Mazel, NY.

Gray, J. (1992) *Men are from mars and women are from Venus.* Harper Collins, N.Y.

Hollis, J. *Eden Project*: http://www.goodreads.com/quotes/tag/individuation (accessed 9-9-16)

Hawkins, D.(1995) *Power vs Force* Hay House, California.

Jantz, G.(2014) *Brain differences between genders*

https://www.psychologytoday.com/blog/hope-relationships/201402/brain-differences-between-genders (accessed 9-9-16).

Johnson, R. (1989) *She: understanding feminine psychology* Harper, N.Y.

Johnson, R. (1991) *Owning Your Own Shadow: Understanding the Dark Side of the Psyche* Harper One, N.Y.

Jung, C.G. (1964). *Man and His Symbols*, Doubleday and Company, N.Y.

McCraty, R. and Childre, D. (2004) "The Grateful heart : The psychophysiology of appreciation" in *The Psychology of Gratitude*, edited by R. A. Emmons and M. E. McCullough. Oxford University Press, N.Y. pp.230-255.

Schnarch, D. (1997). *Passionate marriage: love, sex, and intimacy in emotionally committed relationships.* Owl books, New York.

Schnarch, D., (1991) *Constructing the sexual crucible* Norton, New York.

Sherwood, P (2010) *Holistic counselling: a new vision for Mental Health.* Sophia Publications, Bunbury.

Steiner, R.(2011) *Sexuality, Love and Partnership.* Rudolf Steiner Press, NY.

Steiner, R. (1980) "Man and Woman in the Light of spiritual Science" in *The Anthroposophical Review.*vol 2, no. 1.

Chapter 4:

Childhood shadow karmas: tearing love apart

Burne-Jones, E., 1872-1877 *The Beguiling of Merlin*

> I have never forgotten, and I can't imagine you have, and I've thought of it over the years. It was so good, when it was good, I kept thinking. How could it go wrong?
>
> – Martin, G. *Dying of the Light* http://www.goodreads.com/quotes/tag/lost-love?page=3 accessed 28-8-16

Dr Patricia Sherwood

4. Introducing the Shadow in lover relationships

Conflict between couples is foremost and most commonly due to astral material arising from fears or unmet needs and is characterised by anger, frustration, anxieties and fears. These often arise without warning in the space between the two lovers and, what was apparently an ordinary daily experience, suddenly becomes an unplanned fiery or disturbing moment. Lovers often feel flooded by such a moment, taken out to sea by surprise and overwhelmed by the power of this storm in the space between them that was neither planned nor desired. Astral actions lack a strong element of volition or will. They are driven by instinctual fight/ flight responses. In contrast, shadow experiences between couples are of a different order entirely. The shadow comes with poison's darkness like an arrow aimed and shot at the beloved one to belittle them, attack their moral nature and with the intention to make them suffer. Hatred, revenge, cruelty, self-righteousness, greed, injustice and jealousy are the garments of the shadow and nowhere are they seen more clearly than in the family law courts. Unlike unskilful conflicts arising from the astral, where both parties are victims of their own fears and unmet needs and trapped in the fight/flight response, the shadow is driven by the will located in the frontal lobe of the brain. The shadow is the unacknowledged dark side of the "I" and is formed when one freely chooses to undertake acts that cause suffering and misery to others. Shadow behaviours are calculated acts of hatred, revenge, cruelty or greed driven by will governed only by cold, hard thinking activities. They lack the warmth of the feeling life, which breathes into the will, qualities of generosity, creativity, justice, love, forgiveness, humility and joy in another's joy.

Intimate relationships and the shadow

The disowned shadow

Steiner (1995,p.95) describes will, when warmed by the feeling life, as having profound consequences for human relationships but also for our future, for it is the "seed of what our spirit-soul will become in the spiritual world after death". The long term quality of the union of the "I" and the "Thou" in intimate relationships occurs through moral choices of the will. It is through the will warmed by the feeling life of the heart, that we empathize with and embrace those we love and the world around us. It is through the will, driven by cold, hard thinking that we separate ourselves from our lover, and destroy the person whom we most want to embrace and love. We find fault with them at every turn, not simple criticisms of behaviours but harsh judgments about their moral nature. We start to paint them black and see them as "bad", as opposed to thinking that they are making errors occasionally. Ironically we condemn them for the very moral qualities that we lack, but refuse to acknowledge consciously and own. It is easier and more comfortable to project these moral qualities upon the person closest to us, our intimate lover. Hermann Hesse captured the shadow in action when he commented:"If you hate a person you hate something in him/her that is part of yourself. What is not part of ourselves does not disturb us." Robert Bly (1988,p.17) described the shadow as "the long bag we drag behind us" which is in most lovers the unconscious place in which we store all parts of ourselves we have denied, repressed, disowned, rejected, disliked, or judged as unworthy throughout our lifetime. It is ignored, sealed off like a contaminated radioactive piece of earth that we do not stand upon for fear of what we will have to face and acknowledge about our moral nature. Abraham Maslow (1973,p.54) accurately identified, the part of us that fights to stay in the darkness rather than take responsibility for its moral turpitude. He elaborated upon this which he termed the "Jonah complex" which is the part where "we fear our highest possibilities as well as our lowest ones."

Discovering the disowned shadow in the body

While unprocessed astral material is manifest in the body as functional disorders that form the day-to-day experiences of health issues, unresolved shadow material has sunk deeply into the bodily organs and is reflected in organ disease and dysfunction. The correlation between particular organs and shadow states is summarized in Table 2 below:

Table 2: Organs and associated shadow states

Organ	Shadow state	Antidote
Brain	Pride/self-righteousness	Humility
Eyes	Jealousy	Empathy
Lungs	Revenge	Forgiveness
Heart	Hatred	Love
Kidneys/liver/pancreas	Injustice	Justice
Reproductive organs	Cruelty	Creativity
Bowel	Greed	Generosity

Shadow material is lodged deeply in the body and in the anthroposophical medical model, the karmas of shadow material is borne by the organs. Unresolved shadow material moves from the "I" to the astral, to the etheric, and if it remains unresolved, it settles in the organs. Through death caused by an organ disease, the karmas of the shadow state are finally released from all of the bodies. It is of course more skilful to work on the shadows with one's conscious "I" and to integrate and transform them from the place of insight and awareness. Dossey (1990) in *The Light of Health, the Shadow of Illness* notes the importance of understanding illness as a messenger to the body of the need to deal with material lodged in the shadow and signalling the need to transform it into a dance with the light of good health. The dark shadow is formed in this life as follows: parts of the self that have been repressed in childhood due to the lack of unconditional love by parents underlie a false self that is created to try to be loved. Defence mechanisms are developed in childhood to deny, repress, and sublimate our socially disapproved negative behaviours and this finally results in the disowned self, the negative parts of ourselves that do not receive approval from others (Hendrix, 1990). In the negative dark shadow, these parts represent rejected moral qualities of greed, hatred, injustice, cruelty, revenge, jealousy and self-righteousness/pride. We then choose to believe we are what we are not. We believe we are all goodness and light while denying our dark impulses and behaviours and condemning others for these deeds. We thus avoid taking responsibility for confronting our own shadow. This inauthentic state of existence, Sartre (1992) aptly described as "bad faith" or believing we are what we are not. Intimate relationships are rife with this behaviour if there is no consciousness brought by each person to their unprocessed shadow material.

Discovering unowned shadow material through intimate love relationships

Marriage counselling casework repeatedly demonstrates that the qualities that we value most and which most attract us to our intimate partner, are the qualities that, as the relationship progresses, become the sources of conflict. In time, these qualities are re-envisioned as a result of unowned shadow projections. They now become problematic, bad, negative and even evil and lovers may accuse each other of "having changed" while the truth is probably that the negative unprocessed projections have now surfaced to fracture the dream. So for example, a man may be attracted by a woman's vivaciousness, warmth, creativity and positivity and she, by his reliability, practical competence, and generosity. Further into the relationship, when the shadow rears its head, he is irritated by her passion for life that becomes loudness, her creativity becomes a financial cost, her desire for warmth becomes smothering and burdensome. She may start to re-label his generosity as egocentredness, his reliability as controlling and his practical competence as meanness that he will not call a tradesperson to do a job (Ventura, 1990).

Sharpe (1990) and Ventura (1990) point to the "shadow dancing" that goes on between couples unconscious of the shadow. So for example, one partner can assume the high moral ground of "I never get angry," but provoke the other partner to anger through constant criticism, belittling, nagging or antagonistic deeds or behaviours. The "never get angry person" who represses and denies their own rage, can gain catharsis by his intimate partner's expression of rage, while maintaining the high moral ground and not taking responsibility for their part in the conflagration. In addition, they can hold the self-righteous position of being the "good person" in the relationship while the other person is tainted with drama. This "shadow dancing" can occur with a range of emotions such as sadness, anxiety and procrastination.

Richo (2008) in his insightful work *When the past is present*, identifies how unfinished business with parents will resurface and often sabotage our intimate adult relationships, and cautions us to be mindful of the origins of our reactions to people in the present moment particularly intimate partners as, he emphasises, what we feel has roots in past experiences.

Dr Patricia Sherwood

Mother- father projections onto the marital relationship.

Motherhood projections "anima"

Jung went to great lengths to provide an exposition of how these unowned projections drive heterosexual intimate relationships and cause so much grief, bewilderment and collapse of what was once such intensely owned passionate love. Essentially, the core projection of a man onto a woman contains all of the archetypal qualities of beauty, grace, goodness, nurturing ,creativity, warmth, love, support, compliance, kindness, and loving service. This is represented by the hidden anima in his psyche. Unfortunately, his own anima has been variously wounded by his relationship with his mother, who has shaped his anima. If she was emotionally cruel, cold, self-centred or narcissistic, manipulative or withdrawing, his anima is deeply scarred. As he becomes more intimate with his lover, the archetypal fantasy of the woman drops away and all of these wounded anima qualities will rise to the surface and be projected upon his partner to bear vicariously. He has no idea that he is doing this. He is compulsively blinded by his unconsciousness and unhealed relationship with his own anima, which was shaped by his first primary experience of a female: his mother. The greater the wounding, the more vicious the projection and the condemnation and hate he will project toward his intimate partner and ultimately to all women with whom he becomes intimate. When his hatred colours a woman black and cloaks her with his evil, then he is prepared to burn her at the stake if necessary. He will work compulsively to destroy the relationship and only when he rakes over the ashes, does he realize his desperate unfilled need to connect to a woman mixed with his hatred. Featherston (2016) summarises: "It hurts to breathe. It hurts to live. I hate her, yet I do not think I can exist without her". Unless the man understands the source of it all, his wounded anima from his mother relationship, he is left feeling compulsively confused.

Alternatively, he may resolve this angst by refusing to even try again to create committed intimate relationships. He chooses to become a philanderer and live on the emotional surface of life, never giving his commitment or heart to a woman but simply using her for his own needs, usually sexual. While this may be functional, his anima continues to cry out for help and in his older years his anima will create black moods, sulkiness and discontent within his life. He will ultimately bear the marks of bitterness and defeat upon his countenance.

It is true to say that if one views a man's relationship with his mother and it is fraught with hatred and distrust, an intimate relationship with this man is for a female lover doomed, unless he moves from unconsciousness around his anima to consciousness and he works actively to heal the wounding. Insight into these projections is very liberating although humbling and intimidating for a man. The crumbling of the dream of the perfect lover built upon projections is inevitable, regardless of the intensity of the passion:

> "The day will surely come when one or both of us becomes dissatisfied with this illusion. We will complain that we are misunderstood. Or our beloved will react with rage to the confinement in which our projection imprisons her. She is not the woman we want to believe she is. There is a whole lot more to her. She feels that she has become nothing but our sexual object or our gratifying fancy. If we cannot see her for who she is, she wants to be rid of us…We have not been relating to our beloved at all, but only to the projection we have hung upon her. Our anima or animus has been nothing but a mask which hides our beloved from our sight. Now comes the hard part. We have to "withdraw the projection" in order to see her for who she is" (Haule, 2016)

Transformation and healing are essential. When we withdraw the projection from our lover, we come face to face with the deepest woundings inflicted upon us by our mother's failings. This woundedness is a man's greatest fear. His courage falters as he feels emotionally so vulnerable and exposed but it is the only way to transformation. Otherwise, his relationships with women will remain a litany of brokenness, frustration and despair or superficiality. He will be profoundly defeated in his quest for intimacy.

Fatherhood projections: "animus"

The unconscious side of a woman's emotional life is her animus or male aspect which is encapsulated by the ideal masculine archetype of strength, courage, protection, security, knowledge, rationality and power in the world. Her archetype is of the man who will provide her with protection, leadership, courage, and security in light of the world's vicissitudes. However, her archetype is coloured by her father experiences in childhood because this profoundly shapes her projections onto men in her life. If her father relationship was wounded through rejection, criticism, abandonment, domination, fear, neglect then the relationship with her partner will eventually become coloured by these qualities. The man who originally was her hero, her security, her strength in the world begins to fray at the edges as her projections from her wounded father relationship take over. She begins to criticise him for what she perceives as his weaknesses and starts to lose confidence in the security and strength that she feels he should provide for her in her life. If she does not deal with her unconscious animus needs, she becomes increasingly insecure if she experiences him as failing to provide security and strength for her, or failing to stand between the world's problems and herself. She will become hostile or critical towards the man whom she loves or withdraw her warmth and love and retreat to the corner where her father abandoned or rejected her. In her unconsciousness, she will blame the man for the demise of the relationship. She must heal her wounded animus, or relationship with her father so she can build her own self-esteem and strength in the external world and stand confidently upon her own feet, without requiring her partner for strength. How should women deal with the animus archetype inside them? There is a very important study on the animus written by Jung's wife Emma (1978). She wrote:

> *"What we women have to overcome in our relation to the animus is not pride but lack of self-confidence and the resistance of inertia. For us, it is not as though we had to demean ourselves, but as if we had to lift ourselves."*

Unless women have the courage to undertake this journey in intimate relationships with their male lover, they will continue to experience a series of faltering relationships and witness intimacy crumble before their eyes and continue to complain, "there are no good men in the world".

Dr Patricia Sherwood

Jung, (1925, p.338) summarised the problem of intimate relationships which he believed was innate to the human constitution. He described it as the idealised version of the opposite sex which is projected with all its woundedness by our first relationship with the parent of that gender, onto our lover in intimate relationships:

> *"Every man carries within him the eternal image of woman, not the image of this or that particular woman, but a definite feminine image. This image is fundamentally unconscious; an hereditary factor of primordial origin engraved in the living organic system of the man, an imprint or "archetype" of all the ancestral experiences of the female, a deposit, as it were, of all the impressions ever made by woman-in short, an inherited system of psychic adaptation. Even if no women existed, it would still be possible, at any given time, to deduce from this unconscious image exactly how a woman would have to be constituted psychically. The same is true of the woman: she too has her inborn image of man."*

Only through consciously claiming the problem, examining and healing our woundedness can our intimate lover relationships be rescued from the cauldron of unrealistic expectations and grounded in the reality of human imperfection. We must claim and heal our own shadow in order to rescue our intimate partner from the abyss of relationship projections.

Case studies:

Rachel and Ben

For the first twelve months of their relationship, Rachel and Ben projected the idealised archetype of lovers upon each other. For Ben, Rachel was the kind, warm, caring, sensitive woman who delighted in his presence and was sexually, intellectually and emotionally made for him. Rachel projected onto Ben the idealised father image. He was strong, intelligent and in touch with the world and she felt he stood as her protector between herself and the world. He gave her a sense of security and new-found confidence, especially after having raised two children alone for the previous 14 years.

To understand how such an idealised perfect match can fail, we need to elucidate Ben's relationship with his mother and Rachel's relationship with her father. This will reveal the wounded projections, which were to take the relationship out to stormy seas. Ben's relationship with his mother was unhappy. He described her as the narcissist who ruined his childhood happiness by leaving his father and by deliberately blackening his father whom Ben adored. He hated his mother's manipulation of himself against his father, and what he saw as her sabotaging of his well-being. He resented her pre-occupation with tennis parties, cards, and cocktail events during his childhood. He felt traumatised by the random irrational control she held over his young life. His adult relationship with his mother moved through phases of hostility and withdrawal and then attempts to be caring and gain her approval.

Rachel in contrast, adored her father who described her as, "the apple of his eye," and likewise adored her. Unfortunately though, the desire for closeness with her father was stymied by either his years of work in distant parts of the country which prevented him from seeing her more than once yearly, or by his chronic alcoholism which led him to retreat with his bottle for weeks on end. Her parents separated when she was five years old and she was devastated. Rachel remembers during the weekends sitting on the front fence around her house as a small child, waiting for her father's weekly access visits, which mostly would not occur. She could not tell the time, but she would sit on the fence from sunrise and watch the sun move across the sky all day until sunset. Then she knew her father would not come and she would wander inside broken hearted for her evening meal only to have to listen to her mother repeat her mantra about her father's alcoholism, unreliability, hopelessness and to be reminded by her mother that "they would all be living on the streets if it was left to him to provide". At 8 years of age, Rachel wrote a letter to her father on the other side of the country begging him to come home because she missed him so much and the next year her parents made efforts to reconcile. Her parent's reconciliation was short-lived and her father spent most of his time inebriated and alone with his bottle in the sleep-out of the family home.

It is not surprising that in her adult relationships with men, Rachel chose men who were controlling, who wanted to be with her day and night and fill her body, mind and soul with their presence and demands. These filled the big yawning empty hole of the absent father that she was dragging behind her into her adult relationships. Ben was a perfect match for this need. He was competent, controlling over even minor details like how she cooked, gardened, what she ate, and her dress. Initially, this was very comforting because it gave her a sense of protection and security. He told her how to manage her life and this gave her a sense of a man's strength, power and competence standing between her and the material world. She felt safe in his control and his practical competence. He on the other hand was a master of control, as that was the only way he knew to deal with the threat that women posed to his unconscious wounding by his mother that had left him feeling helpless as a child. He could not afford to feel the vulnerability that he experienced as a helpless child in the face of what his mother's manipulation.

However, by 18 months, the projections of the ideal started to crack and unaware that these wounded childhood experiences provided an unhealthy breeding ground for shadow projections, they entered a stormy period in the relationship. The build up of these unconscious wounded projections of mother and father culminated during a holiday two years into the relationship. Over lunch, he began suggesting properties in the holiday location in which he thought she should invest her superannuation monies rather than leaving it in the bank. Rachel then told him that she had already purchased a small unit with her superannuation fund. He was shocked, then very angry and described her as self-centred, manipulative, a liar, a bitch and a narcissist. At that moment, she had become his wounded mother projection and he was the wounded child whose interests had not been considered by his self-centred mother. He stormed out and went for a long walk which left Rachel in her wounded father projection as the abandoned child, sitting on the front fence waiting for him to return, never knowing just when she might see him again. This incident demonstrates clearly how unresolved family shadows that have wounded our childhoods, destroy our adult lover relationships. Rachel could have considered him, consulted him and perhaps they could have shared a purchase but she retreated to the lonely child who had no support in her life.

Kate and Ian

Kate and Ian had discussed buying a new family vehicle now that they had two children and all that extra baggage to cart around. Kate wanted a station wagon and they had already viewed a few brands. One afternoon Ian arrived home with a 4WD, which he claimed was a bargain purchase. Kate was shocked as she did not like 4WD's and she was the one who would have to drive it most often. She was taken aback by the cost and the fact that the vehicle was not what they had discussed as the required vehicle. They came to counselling following what they described as an "almighty row". Ian was angry and upset because he felt Kate lacked appreciation for all the hard work he had done to save the money to buy the vehicle, while she was on maternity leave with the two children. Her anger and criticism of him, which went on for over one hour, triggered him unconsciously back into the fears he felt as a young child trying to please his very volatile mother who would fly off the handle for the smallest provocation. Kate on the other hand, was trapped in the fear she had experienced as a child with her very authoritarian father who controlled all of Kate's life including what types of sport she could play, what school she could attend and what friends she could visit. She was totally unaware that at the moment that Ian showed her the vehicle he had bought for her that she was triggered back into the feeling of her life being controlled by her father as a small child. Her father had never considered her wishes or interests and now she was facing the same trigger situation in her adult couple relationship, and feeling the same fear and helplessness.

Fiona and Michael

Both Fiona and Michael were very fortunate in that their parents have been present for them in predominately positive ways during their childhoods. Fiona's father had reduced his work to part time when she was born so she had a strong connection with him from her earliest memories. She felt deeply loved and treasured by her father and she recalled how he always encouraged her to try new activities in her life. Michael's relationship with his mother was warm and loving as she had strongly believed in and supported him throughout his childhood even when he did not do well at school. She had always been quietly supportive but tended to remain in the background of the family system.

Fiona and Michael presented in therapy with arguments around employment. Fiona was upset that Michael had thrown in his Telco job and was uncertain about what he would do next in his life. She wanted to settle down and start a family in the next couple of years and he seemed to be lost, and "at sea" without any clear direction as to where he might work in the future. This triggered Fiona back to her childhood fears of insecurity. When her father had lost his job during a restructure of the company, she remembered the anxiety that crippled her mother on a daily basis wondering how to pay the next bills. She was projecting her angst from this period onto Michael who was taken aback as Fiona was usually very supportive of decisions that he made in his life. Fortunately, some career counselling helped Michael to find some new orientation in this life as well as become understanding of Fiona's vulnerabilities around family income which she had brought from her childhood.

Conclusion

The unprocessed shadow projections from our wounded childhood upon our lovers are at best disquieting and at worst toxic. Unless rooted out they will grow as weeds in the relationship, finally choking the land and preventing the growth and healthy nourishment for each other. Passionate lovers who survive the challenges of the wounded childhood projections either have consciousness around what is happening, or they engage in forgiveness and gratitude and accept the limitations of their partner. They scale down their expectations and focus with gratitude on what are the positive gifts in the relationship rather than focus on how their needs are not satisfied by their lover. Such lovers are also capable of giving each other space to make their own decisions on a range of issues, accepting that each person will make different decisions. Enmeshment is the net that suffocates relationships and keeps lovers trapped in wounded projections.

Core to successful long-term passionate lovers is the gradual awakening to, and acceptance that they are the only person who can ultimately make themselves happy and that they are responsible for their own happiness. This involves letting go of expectations that my lover must make me happy and in some unconscious way heal my wounded childhood. As Snider (2013) notes:" people who are not happy with themselves cannot possibly be happy with you"

References

Bly, R. (1988) *A little book on the human shadow*, Harper, San Franscisco.

Dossey, L. (1990) "The Light of Health, The Shadow of Illness" in Zweig, C and Abrams, J (eds) *Meeting the Shadow: the Hidden power of the dark side of Human Nature* Tarcher Press, Loss Angeles,pp91-92.

Featherstone, C.(2016) *Addiction* www.goodreads.com/quotes/tag/lost-love?page1.

Haule, J.(2016) *The Lens of the anima and what it sees*. www.jrhaule.net/ (accessed 12-9-16.)

Hendrix, H.(1990) "Creating the false self" in Zweig, C and Abrams, J (eds) *Meeting the Shadow: the Hidden power of the dark side of Human Nature* Tarcher Press, Los Angeles pp 49-52.

Hesse, H., https://au.pinterest.com/pin/317785317432313008 (accessed 12-9-16).

Jung, E. (1978*)* *Animus and Anima*, Spring Publications, Dallas, Texas.

Jung, C.J. (1925) "Marriage as a Psychological Relationship" In CW 17: *The Development of the Personality*.

Maslow, A.(1973) *The Farther Reaches of Human Nature*. Penguin, Melbourne.

Miller, P. (1992) "What the shadow knows: an interview with John A Sanford" in Zweig, C and Abrams, J (eds) *Meeting the Shadow: the Hidden power of the dark side of Human Nature* Tarcher Press, Los Angeles pp 19-26.

Richo, D.(2008) *When the Past Is Present: Healing the Emotional Wounds that Sabotage our Relationships* Shambala, USA.

Sartre, J. (1992) *Being and nothingness*. Simon and Schuster, N.Y.

Sharpe, D. "My Brother/Myself" in Zweig, C and Abrams, J (eds) *Meeting the Shadow: the Hidden power of the dark side of Human Nature* Tarcher Press, Los Angeles pp 69-71.

Sherwood, P (2012) *Holistic counselling: through the shadow to compassion* Sophia Publications, Bunbury. Australia.

Snider, S. (2013) https://au.pinterest.com/pin/529876712387106162/

Steiner, R.(1995) *Intuitive Thinking as a Spiritual Path* Anthroposophic Press, N.Y.

Ventura, M,(1990) "Shadow dancing in the Marriage Zone" in Zweig, C and Abrams, J (eds) *Meeting the Shadow: the Hidden power of the dark side of Human Nature* Tarcher Press, Los Angeles pp 76-80

CHAPTER 5

Dying in relationship: dark shadow karmas

Everett-Millais, J. (1852) *Ophelia*

> I think it's time I let you go and that's so hard to do because a part of me will be in love with you for the rest of my life.

– Unknown www.//au.pinterest.com/explore/ending-relationship-quotes/

5. Dark shadow karmas

Dark shadow karmas are the accumulation of all our deeds with our lover that are not centred in the light. We could not be passionately attracted to a person or fall in love with someone with whom we do not have past karmas. The greater the passion, the greater the karma and although initially we see the vision of the potential of our meeting in all its glory, over time, the deep and difficult karmas emerge through the processes of energetic vibrational resonances between the couple. These difficult patterns are re-enacted through the current life and its presenting issues unless there are high levels of awareness, which enable the lovers to re-pattern dark karmas into some positive energetic pattern. Everything is energy and events in the current life with resonances to energetic patterns from other times will be brought to the surface between the couple, even if they have no awareness of what is happening. This also provides one explanation as to why couples sometimes find they are going through a dark patch in the relationship without exactly being able to point to external triggers in their current lives.

There are woundings and joys between each person in the couple relationship for ages upon ages. In the present moment, energetically moving between two persons are all the experiences they have ever shared, for the past, present and future are concurrent. It is just that our consciousness of these experiences in other lives is repressed or hidden. During bodily based processes used in Holistic counselling and documented extensively in Sherwood (2012) *Holistic counselling through the shadow to compassion,* the process for opening the parts of the "I" or higher mind that store these memories is explicated. Suffice to say, clients using this model of therapy eventually end up recalling experiences from other times, some persons within the first six sessions while other persons will not recall such experiences until they have completed more sessions. This occurs whether or not clients believe in past lives.

Group soul incarnations

During my clinical work, it has become apparent that people share incarnations in groups and tend to build karmas in groups. We are lovers, partners, friends, relatives, neighbours over and over again. Each meeting is a new opportunity to encounter each other and transform any difficult dark deeds or karma into positive healing karmas. Each new incarnation and meeting may also provide opportunities to enlarge the joy and love that pre-exists between a couple. The notion of group soul incarnation was first brilliantly documented in 1973 by the British psychiatrist and researcher Arthur Guirdham(1991) who documented a compelling case for group reincarnation and produced thorough evidence. He uncovered that a group of his psychiatric clients could recall memories as Cathars in 11th century France and when regressed in therapy could even speak in this ancient French dialogue of Languedoc which is no longer spoken today. They shared experiences of trauma during the heresy purges of the Cathars. They knew each other then and today were all from the same village in Bristol. Newton (2001) in his remarkable clinical work documented in *Destiny of Souls* researched and written in the USA, also points to the processes of group incarnations.

Couple past life karmas and the shadow

These can be of three types: firstly, joyful, positive and caring karmas through whatever challenges the life had to offer with no accumulated shadow. Secondly, there can be lives in which one party of the couple was the victim and the other partner the perpetrator, or, thirdly there can be lives in which both partners were perpetrators. Of course, with all couples, there is a mixture of the above three, but the type of mixture determines how challenging the meeting is in the present life. Shadow therapy with your partner requires great courage and tenacity and is very humbling and liberating because it always reveals no matter how wronged you feel by your partner in this life, you have not always been "white as driven snow". There have always been lives in which you have been the perpetrator. Moreover, it is not all "tit for tat" over past lives. Sometimes there is more "tat tat" than "tit tit" but always there is some of each of these gestures of victim and perpetrator when one uncovers the long expanse of the many incarnations that we have had with our lovers. In fact, so vast is the trail of karmic connections upon this planet and elsewhere, that there comes a time when the lifetimes are beyond easy computation.

Understanding the origins of this past dark shadow in couple relationships.

The obvious question is where has the capacity for evil, that is the antithesis of LIVE (note spelling) originated. Many books of theology and philosophy have attempted to answer this question as to the origin of evil. I am not attempting to summarise these, but rather to present the pictures that clients have revealed in therapeutic processes in which they have regressed to the past. Core themes of experience emerge in descriptions in which clients recall the origin of evil in their past. My clients are primarily secular in belief, although some few have Christian, Hindu or Buddhist backgrounds.

From paradise of Light to the dark shadow

Clients recall a time before shadow states existed, a sort of pristine paradise of light where love, kindness and goodness were the only known experiences. This could equate to concepts variously described in the religious literature as the "Garden of Eden", "the Crystal City", "Paradise". They also recall a slide from this Light, gradually over aons into conditions characterised by the shadow state of greed, hatred, cruelty, injustice, revenge, pride and jealousy. Their descriptions of the originators of the "the fall" or shadow states are reminscent of figures attributed to this process illustrated in art, mythology and religion. The figures who initiated this betrayal into the shadow states of existence, are named in various religious traditions as the "dark angels", "the fallen angels", "the asuras," "the mahasuras", or the "jealous gods". These beings must betray love because having freely chosen to live outside of the light and exchange it for power, they must steal light or energy from the kingdoms of the humans or the gods in order to survive. This is because without light, there is no energy. In Tibetan Buddhism this realm is known as the realm of the jealous gods. It is described "as the realm of the fighting demons, the *asuras*, who, despite being semi-divine, are in a constant state of envy, declaring war on heaven and upon the earth". In the Hindu cannon these beings are known as the asuras or mahasuras who can only be controlled by the force of Durga one of the fiercest emanations of Kali. She is the consort of Shiva and plays significant roles in the creation and transmutation of darkness on a personal and planetary level. In the Hindu understanding of the world, during the epoch when the mahasuras dominated everywhere, there was human misery and suffering, environmental devastation and starvation. The gods had withdrawn up into the high mountains to contemplate the disaster after their defeat. The earth was at the point of extinction. Out of the flames of the mouth of Shiva, Vishnu and Brahma, Durga was birthed. She is symbolic of the ultimate cosmic recycler and transmuter and she alone could defeat the mahasuras. Durga solved the problem of pillaging by these asuras. If they were slain, every drop of their blood as it landed on the earth, would produce a new demon and new asura to further torture humanity. To solve this problem, Durga would lick up and consume every drop of blood of each slain asura, digest and transmute it in her own body and integrate its power for positive creative purposes. She is the flaming symbol of fierce compassion which stops the destruction, protects the vulnerable and ends the war with the shadow (Galland, 1998).

"Eating the shadow," is a metaphor used to describe the depth

Lover relationships and karma

of association needed to transform one's darkness. It simply cannot be chased away because it is part of each one of us. It is not a force attacking us but our own darkness within ourselves that if not transmuted, will become a ferocious force for projecting hatred upon others. It provides the match that ignites wars between each other, between couples and families and even nations. Robert Bly advises that:

> *"One thing that we need to do as Americans is to work hard individually at eating our shadows and so make sure we are not releasing energy which can then be picked up by the politicians, who can use it against Russia, China or the South American countries" (Zwieg and Abrams, 1998,p280)*

Hatred and disconnection

The picture of the quality of the shadow has been pieced together from experiences of clients that have regressed considerably far back into their past lives. They capture the common themes of experience that explain the qualities of the dark shadow. Hatred appears to be the mother of all dark shadow states. The baby of hatred is disconnection from others, the child of hatred is judgment and the adolescent of hatred is condemnation. Following this developmental path at a psychological level, the adult then manifests hatred. Hatred is created out of the belief that one is superior to others and therefore should be separate from the whole and be entitled to better treatment. It is evident everywhere today in narrow nationalist movements that call for the suppression of difference and the repression or removal of those who are not like us. We are the superior or entitled pure ones and those others must be removed, extinguished and excluded from our world because they will contaminate our false purity. The stories of original sin remind us that the cosmic temptation is to leave light so as to acquire special powers just for oneself. Our fall from grace, from the paradise of love, innocence and interconnectedness is reflected in mythologies as a betrayal by those who promised greater power than that which was innately one's inheritance. Love of power is the snake in the garden of our contentment. This was the first slick sales gimmick "you deserve better", "you are superior to those around you and you can be as Gods in the power hierarchy". Of course, hatred goes hand in hand with the shadow of greed, the delusion that "more is better" for oneself, regardless of the cost to others and the environment (Hawkins, 1995).

Jealousy

The snake in the Garden of Eden, entices the unsuspecting to believe that more power is the purpose of existence without revealing that the price for this fast growth product is the loss of connection to the natural rhythmns of our growth and the rhythms of our heart's love which connect us in fulfilling ways to each other. It is the severity of the co-operative, supportive community of existence and the beginning of the hierarchical, linear world of competition where the aim of the game is to get the most power first. This is captured in contemporary slogans like "the man with the most tools wins", "all for me" and "the meek shall inherit the earth, that is what's left of it". Those who miss out must survive as best they can. They are simply road bumps on the pathway to success, and provide opportunties to pillage more power more quickly, rather than earn it through their own inner growth and development in goodness and through expressing compassion as interconnectedness. Fox (1990,p.49) uses the symbol of climbing the ladder to represent the quest for competitive power that produces ruthlessly independent persons, who are jealous and proud at the cost of compassion and interdependence. Hatred and jealousy are the twin pillars of the original perpetrators of the dark shadow.

Bitterness

Another pathway to the shadow is bitterness which comes from the hardening or closing off of the heart as a result of deep feelings of despair and powerlessness and a deep desire to take revenge upon those who have afflicted suffering upon you, or those you love. The downward slide to bitterness is overwhelming, unresolved grief and loss. The person feels that they or those whom they love have been a victim of shadow states of cruelty, hatred, revenge, injustice, greed, jealousy, or pride. The grief and loss caused by this repeated and unrelenting suffering eventually breaks their heart. The person either chooses to go down under the weight of the powerlessness and become despairing and so sinks into the black hole of inactivity or depression, or otherwise resolves to strike back at the source of their suffering in bitterness and revenge. When feeling dominates in a person, they are most likely to go to despair and depression. When the willing attribute dominates in an individual, they are most likely to go to bitterness and revenge. Bitterness is the child of the marriage of despair and hatred who wears the clothes of revenge. In bitterness, the heart is cut off from love and a clearing is made for the downward path to the shadow. Given the opportunity to seize power over the perpetrator, the bitter one will ensure that payback takes place. In bitterness, there is only a desire to get even, or better still, to get ahead. The bitter live in a disenchanted world, moving from one battle to the next. The bitter one becomes caught in an endless cycle of hatred and revenge with their companions of cruelty and injustice. In bitterness there is a refusal to release the memory of the hurt and a resolution, never to "forgive or forget." In bitterness, we generate negative and often deeply cynical attitudes to life. There is a separation from the sense of connectedness with the power of goodness and we believe that we have been abandoned in our hour of utmost need by the Light or by those who should care for us. Shakespeare brilliantly captures this bitter spirit of the dark shadow in King Lear when he writes:"As flies are to wanton boys are we to the gods, they kill us for their sport," a bitter and potent comment on the God's indifference to human suffering. So in bitterness we become a potent link in the chain of shadow behaviours, as there is always a reason to pay back as the seemingly endless cycle of hatred and revenge enmeshes our lives. We live in an heartless desert where there is only bitter water to drink.

Fear of extinction

Fear of extinction is another pathway to the shadow of hatred. The vulnerable heart that is defeated and repeatedly suffers as a victim of the actions of hatred, cruelty and injustice will ultimately feel powerless to protect itself in the face of those onslaughts and attacks and will eventually be unable to endure the fear of extinction, so will resort to hatred as a cloak of protection. Hatred blackens the heart, kills its warmth and creates a dense shell around it which cuts off feelings. This level of fear leads one to make unskillful alliances with perpetrators of darkness in order to survive.

The roots of the dark shadow and its associated karmas lie in hatred, jealousy, bitterness and fear of extinction. We long to find the qualities of love, warmth, kindness, light, beauty and joy in our intimate relationships. Despite all our shadows, the archetype of love, kindness and goodness seems firmly achored within our consciousness and nowhere more clearly manifest than in our quest for intimate relationships. Unfortunately we are all wounded and the perfection we seek cannot be found in another person in the long term, for eventually they shall reveal themselves as human: flawed with a shadow. If couple relationships are to succeed then we must come to terms with our own dark shadows and withdraw them from our partner.

Impact of the dark shadow on couple relationships

The greatest impact that the ungoverned dark shadow has on

couple relationships is to poison the roots of the relationship which will eventually lead to its death. In a person's unconsciousness they blacken their partner with all their unowned darkness, and all the qualities they disown within themselves that they project onto their partner. From the heights of passionate obsession with their image of their partner as their ideal, they reduce them through the fires of projection, with the associated judgment and hatred, to the ashes of extinction. This shifting of their own problem to the interpersonal space with their partner is known in therapy as "projective identification" which is well defined by Scarf (1992,p.71) as:

> "a pervasive, tricky and often destructive mental mechanism which involves one person's projecting denied and disavowed aspects of his or her inner experience onto the intimate partner and then perceiving those dissociated feelings as existing in the partner."

The trigger is always in the present moment but when this experience comes from the past, the ensuing emotional malestrom between the couple always bears an intensity that is beyond the trigger. So for example lets refer to Kate and Ian. He arrives home from work to find Kate chatting to an old male friend who is visiting with his male partner of 10 years. Ian, who is not physically violent, walks into the living room, ignores the visitors, walks out and bangs his fist on the door as he shuts it, damaging the door. He then refuses to talk to Kate that evening. In the presenting moment one could say Ian is upset that Kate is giving her attention to other people instead of himself. This level of response indicates it has past shadow karmas underlying it. Therapy revealed that in a previous incarnation when Kate and Ian were husband and wife, Ian killed Kate, albeit wrongly, for what he suspected was an affair with a neighbour. There was sufficient energetic commonality in the present moment to trigger Ian into his dark shadow. The irrationality of the present moment reaction always indicates that a dark shadow from either a childhood wounding, or a past life is running the show through the couple's unconsciousness. This therapy would also reveal why Kate felt the compulsive need to placate Ian and keep him happy even though she recognised that his reaction to her chatting with her homosexual friends was totally irrational. If we multiply such examples in a couple relationship with the unconsciousness that surrounds them around both their childhood and past life karmas, we start to clearly see why so many lover relationships, particularly passionate relationships drown in the karmic seas between them, and without "I" navigation, partnerships end as wrecks on the ocean floor of their once vibrant love.

Transforming dark shadows from the past : therapeutic interventions

Becoming conscious alone of the dark shadow karmas contaminating a couple relationship is not enough to change them. The energetic pattern of negativity must be transformed from a negative pattern to a positive pattern. If both persons in a couple undertake this process then it is exceedingly beneficial and there are high odds that the couple will survive and move on to flourish. However, when only one person in the relationship is willing to undertake shadow therapy, then the outcome for the relationship is less certain. The therapy will certainly reduce the level of conflict between the couple even if only one person pursues it, but unless their partner takes some responsibility for their shadow too, however they choose to do so, eventually the relationship will most likely fall apart as the responsible person who is seeking to change, grows further and further away from their partner. However, it does mean when the separation occurs, it will not be inflammatory to the same degree as it might otherwise have been. Sometimes, one person taking responsiblibity for their own shadow in a relationship is sufficient to keep the relationship together in a functional manner.

Vows, promises, contracts

An outline of the therapeutic techniques for transforming shadows is documented at length in (Sherwood, 2012) .Firstly, all karmas are caused by intentions and the more powerful the intentions, the stronger the karma. The most powerful core intentions that must be transformed then, are vows, promises, and contracts which continue to transcend the life span in which they were formed. In the initial past meeting with deeply emeshed passionate lovers one usually finds a "divine marriage". This is a time when they came together for great creative acts in the light, a divine marriage which was witnessed by many beings representing the different communities or systems from which the couple originated. The union occurred because together they could complete some creative work in the universe because of their complementary set of skills for that task.

This exchange of gifts, rings, energetic parts of the heart shared in that union have given that couple extraordinary power to access each other energetically. Here we behold the person, who currently distresses us so much, in their original divine stature, before conflicts arose between us. It is essential that the divine marriage and its associated vows, promises and contracts be dissolved. This is because each person is vulnerable to exploitation and appropriation of their light and parts during "the fall into the shadow" because of the exchange of energetic parts that occurred in such marriages. Until our wills and intentions are entirely repolarised with the light of compassion, it is unskilful to allow another person to access us energetically. Each person must return to realign their wills with the light entirely through their own efforts and using their own energetic parts. They cannot ride on the back of another person's energetic parts or system. Everyone must take responsibility for himself or herself, even if they are lovers.

The dissolving vows, promises and contracts sequence has the following steps:

- I hereby dissolve all vows, promises, contracts I have ever made to you voluntarily or involuntarily, individually or on behalf of my people

- You may no longer access me energetically nor may I access you energetically

- I dissolve everywhere in which these vows are inscribed within, without, and in all of the 11 directions and dimensions, to infinity and beyond

- I call back any parts, accoutrements, rings, books of wisdom, or anything else that we have exchanged to keep these vows and contracts in place and send them to the light

- I also dissolve any witnessing, intentions or exchanges of gifts or parts by any other persons that keeps these contracts and vows in place and return all elements and gifts to the light

- I render the power of these vows and contracts null and void in all of the eleven directions even unto infinity and beyond.

- They no longer have any power over my life or any power over your life

- I set you free to take full responsibility for your own well being

- I set myself free to take full responsibility for my own wellbeing.

- I ask that all co-creations be contained within the fiery golden light and be purified and protected therein and realigned in the highest light

This sequence is always deeply moving for the client and followed by a grief and loss sequence because of the intensity of the sorrow about the potential that has been lost and all the destoyed promises in the marriage and the meetings over the ages of shadow encounters. However, it is also a profound opportunity to become compassionate in relation to one's partner, knowing that there is no high moral ground for either of you. Each must bear their own shadow. It is simultaneously both their cross and their redemption.

Calling back missing parts: soul parts

In couple relationships, energetic parts of themself have been exchanged with their lover and the greater the passion the greater the exchange. These parts may have been voluntarily given or involuntarily, consciously given or unconsciously but when clients step into their bodies they will sense these missing parts. We are aware of this in common parlance when we make comments like; "I have given you my heart", I have given you my love", "I have given over my will," or "you have taken my power away." Ask any man after a separation or divorce what parts of himself he experiences as having been taken by his ex-partner and he will have a list. These experiences of missing or transferred parts are so common among couples. In fact, part of their attraction or "love" for their partner is tied into the fact that passionate lovers have many times exchanged parts, voluntarily, or involuntarily as a victim, and we sense these parts of ourselves in the other. In this era of consciousness soul, everyone must rise and fall by their deeds, so it is essential that couples in therapy return each other's parts. This process makes it much clearer as to where the shadows lie. The following sequence is used to return parts

Step 1:

- I hereby remove all parts that do not belong to me and I send them to the highest light.

- I hereby call back all parts of mine that have been taken and I send these parts to the highest light.

- Any parts of others I have taken that do not belong to me, I return to the light

- I ask that collectively all of these parts be cleansed of all inversions, perversions, negativities, curses, codes, negative sound programming, DNA codings, mesmerisings, chippings, inverted sound and light shields, inverted energetic grids and crystalline structures and any yet unnamed or named distortions of the light even unto infinity and beyond.

- I ask that these parts be kept in the highest light and re-polarised in the highest light and reallocated by the highest light to their rightful owners when they can use them with wisdom and compassion for the benefit of all beings

Clients are then asked to step back into their bodies and check that all the missing parts appear to be returning and alien parts have been removed. Clients often experience these parts as a particular colour or shape, not unlike the appearance of precious gems in the colours of rubies, sardius, topaz, emerald, sapphire, amethyst, and diamond. These colours most often correspond to the seven chakras and correspondences to the associated shadow states are documented in detail in Sherwood (2012, pp.94-95).

It is essential to understand when working holistically and energetically that if another person has parts of you or you have parts of another person, then you cannot close your boundaries to them. If we define boundaries as the ability to maintain your personal space in a healthy way so as not to allow yourself to be used or exploited, then an inability to maintain your personal space or boundaries is a serious psycho-emotional problem. Another person only needs one of your parts to have an energetic key to your energy system. When a person is unable to let go of an intimate couple relationship even though it is no longer healthy for either party, one can be certain that they have energetic parts of each other, which are keeping them stuck in the downward spiral. The person being abused will often rationalize this irrational urge to stay and be harmed with comments like: "but I love him/her." Translated energetically it really means "I am in love with my own energetic parts and I cannot leave them behind with this person, no matter what damage this causes the rest of me". Such persons often experience remarkable transformations in their ability to leave harmful relationships after having completed a number of sequences involving the reclaiming of their energetic parts. They are finally able to hold their personal space and leave the unskilful, intimate relationship.

Implants

Clients in couple relationships when dealing with shadow

issues will sometimes find implants in their bodily energetic system, which are geometric structures of varied design often with combinations of patterns, spikes, chords and shapes. As part of the implant structure, there are cords and attachments, which lead to the person who is draining the client of their energy. Implants provide a way of circumventing some karmic laws and allow persons/beings who live in darkness to steal light from persons in the light. The implants drain light energy away from the person who is suffering and into the one living in the shadow while enabling the one living in the shadow to download their darkness and the karmic consequences of their deeds upon the person struggling to live in the light. This elaborate system of injustice and deflection of karmic law is central to maintain the shadow world. Only when beings/persons committed to a life in the shadows are denied access to those struggling to live in the light by the removal of implants, will justice begin to prevail in relationships. Implants are found commonly when there is great oppression in an intimate relationship through violence or abuse and the abused person is unable to leave the relationship, despite repeated assistance from friends, family and professional services.

Implant removal sequence

A brief summary of the steps are as follows:

Step 1

- Ask the client how the implant is fixed to them and have them draw the fixtures, which are often located at the underside of the implant. Each fixture represents one imprint that is a single experience of trauma. If there were six screws, then one would expect to find six imprints of suffering around a common theme holding the implant in place.

- Circle one of the fixtures in gold/yellow crayon according to the preference of the client.

Step 2

- Ask the client to remove the fixture and then draw the shape of the wound left when one of the fixtures is removed. This is the wound wherein is found the imprint of the experience of trauma for that fixture.

- Ask the client to enter into the shape of the wound they have drawn in the full body gesture required to fit into the wound. for example if the wound feels like a slit then one would compress the whole of one's body into a slit like gesture which represents the contracted breathing at the time of the wounding.

- This will reveal the story in the imprint contained within the wound and the appropriate sequences need to be applied to that particular experience of trauma contained within that imprint.

- Complete the processes of the interventions required to heal this imprint using the required sequences such as grief and loss sequence, boundary sequence, betrayal as appropriate.

Step 3

- Repeat the above process for each imprint.

- When all imprints are completed and healed, the attachment either will drop off easily or will have already disappeared.

- Do not remove an entire implant prior to healing each of the imprints as all the range of unhealed imprint traumas may rise to the surface of the client's conscious life and flood them. This causes unnecessary suffering for the client and is of no benefit to the client.

Step 4

- It may take several sessions to complete all the imprints prior to removing the implant.

- Have the client resource themselves after they have completed whole or part of an implant removal sequence.

Calling back shadow parts

When experiencing a shadow and one is in rage, hatred, revenge, cruelty, or pride, couples are often oblivious to the fact that they are sending out an energetic part of themselves that attacks the other person. This is unhealthy for both persons in the relationship: both the person attacked and the attacker and these parts need to be consciously recalled and realigned and purified in the light.

Step 1

- I hereby call back all parts of my hatred that I have sent out to attack and destroy you.

- I call all these parts back and send them to the highest light

- I ask that they be cleansed of inversions, perversion and negativities, curses, codes and any named or unnamed distortions of the light to infinity and beyond

- I ask that these parts be repolarised in the highest light and returned to me for service in the light when I can use them with wisdom and compassion for the benefit of all beings

I forgive myself and seek the opportunity to make restoration for those destructive words or deeds.

Dissolving deals with doubles

When a person explores their shadow in past lives, from time to time they come into contact with their double. One could define one's double as the accumulated intentions to pursue darkness across lifetimes. If a relationship with an intimate has been particularly unjustly oppressive in a lifetime, then it is not unusual to deal with your double to exchange your heart and your love for the power to take revenge upon the perpetrator. Unfortunately this contract continues into your current life and it may cause you from time to time to have very negative thoughts towards your partner. These need to be cleared so that the space between couples is maintained as wholesomely as possible.

The double transformation sequence

- The sequence has the following steps:
- I hereby dissolve all vows, promises and contracts I have ever made with you voluntarily or involuntarily especially the contract to give you my heart in exchange for the power to take revenge.
- I call back any parts or accoutrements or anything else that we have exchanged and send them to the light
- I render the power of these contracts null and void in all of the 11 directions even unto infinity and beyond
- I dissolve all intentions and intentions behind intentions including any of my intentions that have created this form of the double and which keep it in place
- I send all elements of these intentions to the light to be cleansed in the light, repolarised in the light and recycled in the light for use according to the purposes of the highest light
- I affirm that my will is realigned with the light. I am safe and protected in the light and I manifest my power and potential in the light.

Past life review sequence

At the end of each life time, we undertake a life review just after death and this is an incredibly powerful karmic moment when we make a summary intention about our experience in that life. If we lived as a couple and there was trauma in the relationship and we make an intention like: "Next time I'll make him/her pay for what they have done to me" or "I always lose them to some-one else", this will travel on to future lives and meetings and continue to outplay until the intentional energy is depleted. All of these sticky intentions needs to be cleared when one has entered a past life. They undermine the current couple relationship. The sequence is as follows and is done after the client has stepped into the imprint or embodied experience of that life and recalled their relationship intention for that life:

- Go forward to the moment just after your death and point to where you go when your body dies. Clients usually point upwards but sometimes to the side or even downwards or just next to their dead body

- Go and stand in the place where you go after you die (if it is in the air use a chair for them to stand on to simulate the experience of being up in the air)

- Look at your life and find out what you have resolved about that life when you reviewed it. In particular note your summary statement or resolution about that life. Dissolve it if it is unskilful.

- The following is an example if you found hatred or the desire for revenge toward your current partner:

- I hereby dissolve the intention that: "You will pay for making me suffer"

I render the power of this null and void in all of the eleven directions and dimensions even unto infinity and beyond. I set you free to take responsibility for your own well being. I set myself free to take responsibility for my own well being. I affirm; I am free to forgive and to create skilful future relationships.

Reconnection to the light

All trauma experiences with a partner when exploring past shadow lives involve separation from the light and one's source of strength, either as victim or perpetrator. The following sequence is used to affirm the positive new vibrational patterns after completion of the required previous sequences. It is essential that the client reconnect to the light of their "I", their highest and most skilful self.

Step 1:

- experience of abandonment by the light transformed to an experience of reconnection to the light
  "I am reconnected to the light"

- experience of fear transformed into a bodily experience of safety
  "I am safe and protected in the light"

- experience of powerlessness transformed to an experience of power to manifest one's full potential as a human being
  "I am free to manifest my full power and potential and flourish in the light"

Not all of these sequences listed above will be required in every session. Also additional sequences not outlined above may be required. I have only included the most commonly occuring sequences in couple therapy.

Case studies

Rachel and Ben

An example of passionate love that becomes dark shadow material occurred when Ben's daughter and her husband and children were visiting. Rachel provided a meal for the visitors. After his daughter, her spouse and children had departed, Ben accused Rachel of trying to make his daughter "fat and ugly" by serving up too much on her plate. Rachel was shocked as it was not her intention to do anything of the kind. She thought she had been a generous and kind hostess but to defuse the situation she apologised immediately and said it would not happen again. Ben however was sliding rapidly into one of his dark shadow black moods and continued for the next two days and nights to accuse her of lying, manipulating, and undermining his daughter's well being. On the third day, Ben continued to complain in the car on the way to work and finally Rachel asked him to let her out of the car so she could walk the rest of the way to work. He refused and Rachel became possessed with her own dark shadow and smashed the car window. She was shocked and mortified that she could behave in this destructive way, not ever having damaged things before in rage. She apologised and paid for the repairs. This is a typical, albeit graphic illustration of the dark shadow from the past, at work in couple relationships. The "food serving offence" does not justify two days of admonishment nor does the two days of admonishment justify damaging the car window. This is a red flag to a deep dark past life karmic shadow. Rachel presented in therapy suitably mortified and shamed. She went back to a past life when her current partner had been a ruler and had her tried and condemned to death for having failed to take sufficient care of the part of his estate for which she was responsible. On death, her life review sequence was "to avoid and escape from him at all costs in future lives" as she felt unjustly condemned. It needs to be pointed out that such as resolution is as sticky and karmically reconnecting with the perpetrator, as "I hate him and next time I will kill him." Resolutions based in aversion or desire, will still work to reconnect the persons in conflict. It is important that the resolution be "not sticky" such as, "I can choose skilfully whom to serve in the future and whom not to serve". A satisfactory intention would have been: "I will choose skilfully in the future whom to serve and whom not to serve"."

Kate and Ian

An excellent example of dark shadow karmas outworking in this relationship, occurred when Ian came home one evening after a difficult and challenging day at work. He was displeased with the meal Kate had prepared and unceremoniously proceeded to throw his meal in the bin and leave the table. Kate was very angry and responded by selecting an high quality bottle of his favourite wine and pouring it down the kitchen sink. Ian was furious and Kate was defiant and unapologetic. In therapy, this led to a perpetrator to perpetrator past life shadow. In that life, both Kate and Ian were both male generals in competing armies and there was a battle in which they fought viciously until they both had wounded each other so severely that they both died of the wounds. Kate and Ian's resolutions during their respective life review sequences was essentially similar: "I'll get you next time and make you suffer for causing my death". Such a resolution transits lifetimes and had emerged in their 21st century kitchen over a simple meal. To clear this lifetime of hatred and revenge towards each other would require several therapeutic sequences including, the divine marriage dissolution, calling back one's own parts and shadow parts, dissolving deals with doubles and reconnecting to the light . If only one person is willing to own their shadow from the past and become aware of it and they complete the sequences alone, it will still sever the ongoing destructive cycle in future meetings, but more sessions will be required than if both parties in the relationship work on their own shadows.

Fiona and Michael

Our blessed couple, Fiona and Mchael, carrying little family shadow karma nevertheless, did present in therapy with an issue that led to dark shadow karmas. Fiona had become jealous of Michael's receptionist at his new workplace. Now she was at home most of the time with the children, she accused him of flirting with his new, in her view, very attractive receptionist.

He claimed that although she was attractive it was nothing more than a work relationship. Fiona refused to believe this and without any hard evidence continued to create a mental world view in which the new secretary was plotting to have an affair with her husband. She started to demand Michael no longer attend any office social functions and eventually Michael found the control untenable and Fiona the jealousy overwhelming, and they presented in therapy. Eventually, a dark shadow situation emerged in Fiona's therapy when she recalled being wealthy and married to a person whose energy resembled Michael. She had married below her station in life and she treated Michael like a servant although he was her husband. He then began an affair with one of the household servants whose energy of course, resembled the current receptionist. In rage in this previous lifetime, she had Michael and the servant girl caste out of her household onto the streets where they both died penniless. She died of a broken heart and her resolution was: "I must never let him near another woman again when I am his wife". Michael recalled that same situation in his therapy and his resolution was: I must always conform to my wife's demands or I will lose her love and die". Both of these resolution are sticky and continue the dark shadow cycle going onto future lives. Through a series of sequences including past life review sequences, we transformed these intentions into positive intentions: "I can love Michael and be secure and happy" and "I can love Fiona and trust in her love for me." Together with a range of other sequences relating to Jealousy and outlined in Sherwood (2012), the situation was transformed energetically and Michael and Fiona were able to move forward constructively and with trust in their relationship with each other.

Conclusion

The intricacies of the dark shadow karmas that weave through so much of our past life experiences are so easily lit aflame by triggers in the present life because of similarities in vibrational resonance. They come from the past and may contaminate our most passionate intimate relationships. If we don't face our shadow both at the childhood level and eventually at the past life level, our intimate love relationships are at the mercy of the projections arising from the toxic, unacknowledged shadow that resides within us all. It takes courage and humility and strength to face it and self-forgiveness and courage to own and transform it. It is not a task for the faint-hearted. But if we do not take up the task it will eventually poison some of our deepest loves. We can run from relationship to relationship in pursuit of the mythical dream of the perfect lover who meets all our needs, but at the end of the day, we run with our shadow and, unacknowledged and unexplored, it remains a time bomb ready to blow up our dearest dreams again. Jung captures the challenge:

> *"There is no coming to consciousness without pain. People will do anything, no matter how absurd in order to avoid facing their own soul. One does not become enlightened by imagining figures of light but by making the darkness conscious." (Jung, p.99).*

References

Bly, R (1991) *Eating the shadow* Zweig,C. and Abrams, J., *Meeting the shadow: 'the hidden power of the dark side of Human Nature* Tarcher, Los Angeles. pp279-280.

Fox, M (1990) *A spirituality named compassion*, Harper and Row, San Francisco.

Galland, C (1998) *The Bond Between women: A journey to fierce compassion.* Hodder, Sydney.

Guirdham, A (1991) *We are one another.* Newcastle publishing company, Newcastle. U.K.

Hawkins, D (1995) *Power vs Force: The Hidden Determinants of Human Behaviour* Hay House, California.

Newton, M., (2001) *Destiny of Souls.* Llewellyn Publications, St Paul, MN.

Jung, C., (1968) Psychology and Alchemy in The Collected Works of C. G. Jung, vol 12, Princeton University Press, Princetown.

Scarf, M., (1992) "Meeting our opposites in husbands and wives" in Zweig, C and Abrams, J (eds) *Meeting the Shadow: the Hidden power of the dark side of Human Nature* Tarcher Press, Los Angeles pp 72-76.

Sherwood, P. (2012) *Holistic counselling: through the shadow to compassion.* Sophia Publications, Bunbury, Western Australia.

CHAPTER 6

The aftermath karmas: grief, despair and hatred

Blake, William (1812) *Jerusalem Plate* 51(mk47),

" It's a certain tragedy when agony and resentment are all you have left connecting you to someone you once loved. "

— Morse, J. *Now and at the Hour of Our Death* http://www.goodreads.com/quotes/tag/lost-love?page=

Dr Patricia Sherwood

6. The shattered dream

When the intimate, love relationship fails for a lover, it is the shattering of the Dream of finding someone who will meet your expectations and needs. It is at the deepest level, the failure of one or both parties to take responsibility for their childhood or past shadow karmas and transform them into health. Mostly intimate relationships reach this tragic end not because either party is intentionally malicious in this life, but because of ignorance, delusion and projections which are the vehicle for hatred. There are no classes on the dynamics of intimate relationships at school, very few family models of successful intimate partnerships, and with increasing family breakdowns, working parents, and time poor families, there is an abundance of wounded children whose needs are not being addressed. It is not surprising then that the statistics are rapidly rising for divorces in western countries, and most people will have had at least three to four intimate relationship of more than a year by the time they are 65 years of age. While the internet promises fast match making, it also supports the delusions that intimacy promises heaven upon earth, when the reality is that intimacy awakens the wounded hells within you and confronts you with the need to transform them into the heavens within yourself. No one else can do it for you. To blame your intimate partner for your own unhappiness is a downward spiral for intimate relationships.

As the relationship crumbles and descends from the promise of heaven to the harsh realities of 'breaking up", not only the physical separation of possessions and children, if they exist, have to laboured through, but also intense emotional states: grief and loss, despair, bitterness and at its worst hatred and revenge. These difficult shadow emotional states often surface as darkness in the surface issues of the settlement of property and children. Everyone suffers because they are not acknowledged or transformed. If they are not, they weave their venom around children and law courts in a soul destroying way, building in the process, darker karmas for the next meeting with the ex-partner in the next life. How to clear ongoing negative karmas with this ex-partner is the focus of this chapter. One wants to ensure that the relationship has not been wasted, that there has been learning; the acquisition of some wisdom and the release of difficult karmas from the past so they do not re-occur again. It is also essential to deal with one's dark shadows, from childhood in particular, so that they do not undermine any future meetings in new relationships in the present life.

Impact of intimate relationship breakup on the bodies of intimate partners.

On the most fundamental level of brain science, broken lover relationships trigger the brain to light up in the intense physical pain area, even though the pain is emotional. Kross (2016) completing research on couples that had recently broken up noted: "We found that powerfully inducing feelings of social rejection activate regions of the brain that are involved in physical pain sensation, which are rarely activated in neuro-imaging studies of emotion.'(http://www.heysigmund.com/

your-body-during-a-breakup/). Essentially emotional pain and physical pain share the same neural pathways in the brain, so it is not surprising that one feels physically and emotionally depressed and oppressed following a break up with an intimate partner. In addition to the physical body, the emotional bodies suffer significant trauma during the breaking up process.

Breaking up, especially when the relationship has been two years or longer and the intimacy has been intense and strong, is a very painful process for the subtle bodies as well. The breakup is literally a tearing of their energetic bodies of the partners, and their children, if they have any. During an intimate relationship, the etheric body, or life force, carries the emotional streams for a co-joint etheric body with the lover. This co-joint energetic systems can be observed, in that it produces connectedness energetically and ultimately a similarity in lifestyle habits. It is often observable that long, long term couples start to look like each other. When a couple separate, this cojoint energetic system is torn and it bleeds energy which is experienced as "a bleeding heart". Upon an intimate relationship breakup a client will often state that they feel "torn apart", or that "their energy feels like it is draining away". Men and woman in heterosexual relationships experience the etheric, which is of the opposite gender to the physical body, differently. Men experience the etheric as feminine and feel gutted, and emptied out. It is difficult for them to feel stable and together. Women, on the other hand whose etheric is masculine, experience being exposed after a relationship breakup and vulnerable to the storms of life and the vicissitudes of the world. The tearing apart and re-healing as separate etheric bodies takes a prolonged period of time. By one year, the drain of energy is completed but it is usually a two year cycle to feel completely normal again. Entering new relationships during this period is not skilful as one is not in a clear energetic space to accurately perceive the quality of the new relationship. One is often driven by a need to feel whole again, instead of feeling fragmented or torn.

The astral body following separation becomes turbulent with all its experiences of grief and loss, despair, loneliness and sometimes betrayal. This potent brew of feelings is stirs up all resonant energetic patterns of despair, rejection, loneliness, relationship failure, grief and loss that as yet have not been transformed in the lovers' personal life. If a person has an abundance of unprocessed material stored around these core issue then depression, despair and other unhealthy mental states may surface that were previously dormant. This is because the stored astral "traumas" are now overflowing and flooding the person.

The "I" has some choices. Either the "I" takes courage and strength and works with the emotional traumas of grief and loss, rejection, loneliness, and self-blame, to insightfully integrate them into new experiences, or it chooses to enlarge its shadow states with hatred, bitterness and revenge. This second choice will create a potent brew for suffering of self and others, not only in this life but in future lives. The "I" plays the most powerful role in working with the difficult karmas of broken relationships to ensure that wisdom is distilled from the experience. Only when one can move to a position when they are no longer feel recrimination or judgment towards their ex-partner, regardless of their behaviours in the past, are they truly free. One needs to be able to feel nonjudgmental compassion for them as a human being with their own journey limitations and challenges. This means totally letting go of the need to fix them up, change them, blame them or criticise them for past behaviours. This is the position of equanimity, of fully breathing and of allowing the person to be as they have chosen to be. It is very difficult to reach these goals for the "I," because of all the past karmas that keep us energetically enmeshed with ex-lovers, even after we have separated. The greater the initial passion, the vaster and more intense the past karmas.

Transforming grief and loss

Grief and loss in western culture is so ignored and repressed that we scarcely allow ourselves these feelings at all and try to cover them with acceptable feelings like judgment, anger, or hatred towards that person. Underlying all of these negative states after relationship breakup, is profound grief and loss, if only we would go there. We have lost the dream, lost the person in which we invested so much of our time and energy, lost the hopes and shared dreams, lost the memories of the good times. We are triggered by this loss into all the losses of energetic resonance in this life and past lives. For a woman, losses of the father figure of protection and of security underlie so much of her grief. For males, losses of the mother figure, the nurturer, the carer are poignantly painful. The list of losses is pervasive and the etheric body which carries the emotional life streams needs to process these losses while it itself is in a state of bleeding energy. Without question, the first year of the loss is extremely painful. Lost memories are triggered every time an event occurs, or one stands near a place that one shared with one's ex-partner. The memories of things they loved, events you would have shared with them come rolling like waves upon the beach of the battered heart. This is normal, albeit distressing, for two years. The pain gradually subsides by the end of the second year, if one undertakes the transformative work to heal the wounded heart. Otherwise, the pain mounts up and becomes even more intense with the next loss, or the next broken relationship. This is when some people give up, close their hearts and go into future relationships with a perfunctory utilitarianism. They protect themselves from growth and from pain by investing very little of their emotional life in the next relationship, and simply being "there for the ride" when it suits them. Not dealing with one's grief and loss does not help, for time does not heal it. Grief will remain in the energetic system of the etheric, astral and "I" until active conscious healing is undertaken. Breathing fully into the place of grief, and breathing back qualities that have been lost through self-nurture and self-care is healing. Engaging in creative activities such as the arts, gardening, and crafts also facilitate the expression of grief and loss, and its healing. This task must be undertaken because otherwise it becomes another dirty dish in a pile of dirty dishes stacked within your energetic system until eventually you are flooded and one day collapse, physically or mentally, with illness or depression.

Honouring the good

It is essential in grief and loss recovery to remember the good things and to create a gratitude process that celebrates what was good and wholesome in the relationship and which can continue to be remembered. Ex-lovers to whom one was passionately attracted never disappear. You will meet them again, the question is just where and when? The greater positive, skilful, energetic patterns you form out of the alchemists' purifying fire of grief and loss, purifying your own soul and mental space, the more productive the future meeting will be in all its dimensions.

Art therapy exercises using clay are documented by Sherwood (2004) *the Healing Art of clay therapy* and using watercolour in Sherwood (2008) *Emotional Literacy: the heart of classroom management* are excellent for transforming feelings of grief and loss.

Transforming hatred and revenge

"And he hated himself and hated her, too, for the ruin they'd made of each other."

Lehane, D. The Given Day *http://www.goodreads.com/quotes/tag/lost-love?page2*

The first and original inversion of love is hatred, the desire to destroy the person that one loved through causing them as much suffering as possible. This can be daily witnessed in family law courts around the country as one or both vindictive partners fight, not for what is just or in the interests of their children, but for means to destroy, blacken and besmirch their ex-partner or lover. Even in the minds and hearts of those who do not outwardly express their hatred, its seeds fester. Every time one wishes ill-will to an ex-partner, or denigrates them to others, one is manifesting the seeds of hatred. It is essential that these be rooted out, so they do not provide the karmas for future interactions in this life or others. Processes for dealing with hatred involve shadow therapy processes previously outlined. Most of all, one needs the courage and strength to face one's own shadow in relation to an ex-lover. Hatred will not simply disappear in time, but rather, it will sink into the energetic layers of the astral, etheric and "I" causing physical or mental dis-ease down the track.

Revenge is a shadow state like hatred and is extremely toxic. It separates us from our own light and the light of others. It provides a defence mechanism against the vulnerability of our heart. Revenge is one response to unbearable suffering, prolonged grief and loss, and unremitting soul pain. We feel trapped and powerless, caught in a web of suffering inflicted upon us and our loved ones by uncontrollable destructive forces and persons. In the face of such suffering and such injustice, we give up on forgiveness because our energetic system is contaminated by these forces. We are unable to keep them out because of our energetic weaknesses, and so we feel fearful and exposed. It becomes a survival script, of "us or them". We choose revenge, at the cost of our own hearts, and we rationalise it, by saying that we choose to fight the good fight, to stop the persecutor by giving them a dose of their own medicine. In our ignorance and blindness we call it a provoked attack which justifies striking back at them. They will pay and pay, for they must suffer as we suffer.

Revenge rather than forgiveness is the core shadow state presenting in therapy among many divorcing couples. Revenge underlies issues of anger and despair, even when it is covered by expressions about forgiveness. It is easily evoked in the body by simply asking any client who is posturing as a victim: "If you had the power what would you do to effect justice and pay them back for the wrong they have done to you?" Within minutes, the victim's shadow emerges in the therapy room as perpetrator par excellence wanting to smash, hit, bash, burn, and in some way destroy the perpetrator and/or their possessions. Gestures of hatred and revenge upon another human being are projections of our own shadow. Other persons must be punished so that the the sufferer can feel safe, secure and hold their tattered heart in a fearsome container.

Riding upon our self-righteousnes and sanctimoniousness, we effect justice according to our own world view. Revenge gives the illusion that hatred can be countered by hatred, but the karmic result is always more enmeshment between the oppressed and the oppressor. They are caught in a karmic cycle of suffering ,in some lives as the victim, in other lives as the perpetrator. Revenge, however, provides a false shield against the heart's grief and loss, a delusionary world in which we convince ourselves that this fight will be the last fight and the enemy will be vanquished forever. Of course we do not own that the first enemy is in our own heart and mind. There can never be outward victory over hatred and revenge until there is first inward victory over the shadow of hatred in our own hearts and minds. We can only break out of the cycle of hatred and revenge in the degree to which we first discover and forgive our own perpetrator.

Overcoming Buber's I-Thou split is the great psychological and spiritual movement required to enter into forgiveness and compassion. this process calls one to see the other person as a "Thou" a part of divinity like yourself, and not as an "it" or object without spirit or feeling (Buber,1971). It requires sitting with the pieces of our hearts, knowing that ultimately all hearts are connected but we need first to heal our own hearts to become whole. It is knowing that within all hearts there is a story of suffering and survival. As Henry Wadsworth Longfellow(Zweig and Abrams, 1999:194) stated:

If we should read the secret history of our enemies, we should find in each man's life sorrow and suffering enough to disarm all hostility.

Revenge is a great distraction from sensing one's heart because it provides the perfect active diversion from focusing on our own heart's pain which is so intense when intimate lover relationships break apart. Revenge is a spent currency, the real currency is the cost of working to restore, heal, cleanse and enliven our own hearts. Revenge is nothing more or less than an emotional heart bypass. The greater the revenge, the greater the number of heart bypasses we have elected to take. Instead of living from compassion, we choose to live from the will, cold and cruel in its actions when it is severed from the heart. Alternatively, we may choose to live from the mind, hardened and judgmental, moralistic and self-righteous which is severed from the heart's warmth and vitality. Ironically, we direct our darkest revenge to those whom we have once most loved. It takes profound insight and "I" engagement, and an understanding of karma to be willing to step out of revenge and hatred, particularly when one feels that one has been unjustly treated by an ex-lover or partner.

Transforming despair, self-blame and shame

Despair cuts deeply into the "I"s strength and light, for it is the gesture of feeling defeated at the most fundamental level of one's spirit, giving up on the will to live, and giving up on the desire to manifest one's light in one's life. While depression is a collapse of the life rhythms in the etheric body, despair cuts much deeper. It is the loss of purpose and vision held by the "I". When a relationship break up between partners is intense, and a person falls into despair, they are vulnerable to giving up on life entirely and either committing suicide, taking numbing drugs prescribed or otherwise, withdrawing into hopelessness or disengaging in some other way from life and love. When coupled with self-blame or shame in which the person feels that they are in some way responsible for the relationship breakup because of an affair, lack of commitment or something else, it becomes a potent, toxic brew for the despairing one to swallow. It is at these moments that one needs to draw upon one's "I" to connect with other human beings that we know or have heard about who also should be in despair but have transformed that despair into hope: Nelson Mandela, Mother Theresa, Martin Luther King, Gandhi, and the Dalai Lama just to name a few. Meditating upon receiving hope from them and breathing it in on a daily basis can go a long way to reviving one's own "I", and transform our breathing from despair to hope.

Transforming bitterness and betrayal

> *"I think anyone who opened their heart enough to love without restraint and subsequently were devastated by loss knows that in that moment you are forever changed; a part of you is no longer whole. Some will never again love with that level of abandon where life is perceived as innocent and the threat of loss seems implausible. Love and loss, therefore, are linked."*
>
> Hope., D http://www.goodreads.com/quotes/tag/lost-love

Bitterness can be a response to intimate relationship breakdown as a result of the experience of the betrayal of trust and innocence. Bitterness afflicts the "I" with the shadow of cynicism and imploded anger and hatred. The person does not act out in deeds their hatred and anger but it implodes within their energetic system creating a toxic bed that contaminates any future love relationships. Bitterness is a heart shrivelling, mind desiccating state of existence that keeps one's heart safe but lonely. It is a self-made emotional prison with strong steel bars and is writ upon the countenance of the bitter one who has an "upside down smile". Again, until the betrayal is released, the trust rekindled and the grief and loss re-encountered for healing, the person remains trapped in a downward karmic spiral doomed to have another painful, shadow experience, next time they encounter their ex-partner or even a similar relationship.

Case studies

Ben and Rachel separated with tears and grief on both of their parts. They just gradually fell apart until Rachel no longer returned to Ben's house and they were left only with the ashes of their passionate love affair. Ben felt he had given it his best shot, given her his heart and his commitment and concluded that she was in some way flawed. However, the unresolved shadow materials from his childhood and past which were projected into the relationship with Rachel do not disappear. They wait for however long it takes, this life time or another, to rear their ugly heads again and play havoc with his quest for intimacy. Rachel, on the other hand, chose to work initially on her grief and loss for some months and as she became stronger in herself, she decided to work on her reactions in the relationship which had contributed to the relationship crisis. She worked over several therapy sessions on her despair, her self-blame, and her bitterness until she was able to transform these in therapy and return to her positive, optimistic self. She was determined that the shadow karmas of this life or future lives should not repeat in her future intimate relationships. She wanted to live in a clear, peaceful place. In her heart, she remembered Ben's goodness, his strength, his intelligence and his gifts to her life and she cherished these as the good memories to take forward into her life.

Kate and Ian continued to come to therapy and become aware of their childhood karmas that would undermine their relationship from time to time. They were committed to working to maintain their family and to create a better quality relationship with each other and have remained together.

Fiona and Michael have remained together and are fortunate in that they have inherited few family shadow karmas. They are alert though, for dark shadow karmas and on the odd occasions when they sense their level of conflict is beyond the trigger, they take responsibility to understand and clear it as a couple. The long term prognosis for this couple is excellent.

Closure: Is it possible?

Closure with a passionate intimate lover is energetically very difficult to achieve in this life because of the intensity of the karmas between lovers, including both good karmas and shadow karmas from many lives. The ideal scenario is for both partners to work to clear their dark shadow material even when the relationship has finished, as this creates a clear space for the next meeting, whenever that will be. One thing is karmically certain; there will be another meeting in another life until the issues are entirely resolved energetically. If only one person works to clear their dark shadows and withdraw them from the relationship, it will help considerably to keep the relationship out of difficulties in the immediate present life. It also will help to alleviate the destructiveness of the dark karmas in future lives. However, this will not be as effective as when both parties take responsibility for their shadow. The shadow is like a sticky web but if you both free yourself then in future the karmas will be good for intimacy. If only one person frees themself from the web, then their karmic options in the future have widened considerably with that partner. Furthermore, they have loosened the web for their ex-partner to make some changes to release themselves from their own shadow and their co-joint shadow with each other. The least preferred scenario is for both parties to ignore the shadow transformation work and to act it out in this life in long drawn out court battles or social /financial battles. This then digs the hole deeper and upon their next meeting the web thickens and they have deeper darkness into which to descend.

We can leave intimate relationships but the imprints remain energetically and eventually must be transformed karmically, in the long expanse of lifetimes. In essence: "It is hard to forget someone who gave one so much to remember" Unknown http://16quotes.com/hard-to-forget-someone/ because the "unfinished business" remains imprinted energetically, like a saved file waiting to be opened at the next karmic meeting.

References

The Abbotts (2012) Divorce & Separation: The Spiritual Approach to Relationship Breakdowns epub https://books.google.com.au/books?id =2ipcCAAAQBAJ&printsec=frontcover&dq=relationship+breakdown+books&hl=en&sa=X&ved=0ahUKEwjMi6C (accessed 26-9-16)

Buber, M. (1973) *I-Thou*, Free Press, Hudson River, Canada.

Kross, E. *Hey Sigmund Your body during a breakup: the science of a broken heart.* http://www.heysigmund.com/your-body-during-a-breakup/ (accessed 15-9-16)

Hope, D. http://www.goodreads.com/quotes/tag/lost-love (accessed 28-8-16.)

Lehane,D. *The Given Day* http://www.goodreads.com/quotes/tag/lost-love?page2 (accessed 14-9-16)

Sherwood, P. (2004) *The Healing Art of clay therapy* ACER, Melbourne

Sherwood, P. (2008) *Emotional Literacy: the heart of classroom management* ACER, Melbourne

Sherwood, P. (2012) *Holistic counselling: through the shadow to compassion.* Sophia Publications, Bunbury, Western Australia.

Zweig, C and Abrams, J (eds) *Meeting the Shadow: the Hidden power of the dark side of Human Nature* Tarcher Press, Los Angeles.

Chapter 7:
The karmas of light and darkness in relationships

Waterhouse, John William, (1905) *Apollo and Daphne*

> The real meaning of enlightenment is to gaze with undimned eyes upon all darkness

– Kazantzakis, N http://www.brainyquote.com/quotes/keywords/darkness.html

7. The karmas of light and dark in relationships

The karmic view of the energetic flows in intimate relationships can be summarised by elucidating the balance of light and dark, within and between couples. Light is energy, darkness is the absence of energy. Light comes from the universal source of light and is breathed into our bodies moment by moment, day by day. Every healthy cell of our body is permeated with light. In the east, this light energy would be called "prana" or life energy, which comes from the great mahaprana, the cosmic source of energy (Sachedeva, 2012). The sun is the source of light in our solar system and the Divine is recognised as the source of light in many religious cosmologies.

Light is the source of life and love. Darkness is the absence of light and results in disease, ill health and an absence of life force or energy. The vibrational rate of different states of light energies has been researched and measured by Hawkins (1995) who identified energy fields around persons vibrating at different energy ranges depending on their frequency. The lower the ranges of vibration the more negative the thinking states and the lower the light energies. The higher the vibrational patterns of the individual's energy field, the higher the positive emotions and the greater the light intensity. McCraty et al (2006) at the HeartMath institute demonstrates clearly that particular emotional states of depletion and negativity profoundly affect the hearts rhythm, producing incoherent patterns of energy that deplete energy for the individual:

Lover relationships and karma

> 🌙 *"... our research has shown that negative emotions such as frustration, anger, anxiety, and worry lead to heart rhythm patterns that appear incoherent—highly variable and erratic. Overall, this means that there is less synchronization in the reciprocal action of the parasympathetic and sympathetic branches..."* (Mc Craty et al. 2006, p.9)

Being charged with energy is what we all long for in a wholesome and balanced way. We want to feel alive, ready to encounter life with our full potential. The natural source of energy is light. We are all attracted towards the light, towards that which promises us happiness, energy and an enlivening experience of the world within and around us. Love, of course, is one of the great manifestations of two energy fields that touch each other at a vibration that is arousing and attractive to both parties. This merging of energy fields or light resonance occurs when we are in love and is particularly accelerated by sexual intimacy, as outlined in the early chapters.

However, lovers meet with differing combinations of light and dark vibrational energy patterns which are an accumulation of dark shadow experiences across lifetimes and family shadow patterns from this life time as well as accumulated experiences in this lifetime. Each individual vibration in the couple linkage will be different. We could call this vibration their light quotient. When couples have similar light/darkness quotient then the relationship has an excellent chance of enduring in the longer term. When there are substantial differences in the light quotient, other deeper shadow karmas are dominating the processes of energetic attraction. This has profound ramifications for the initial attraction and it results in serious ongoing challenges in the relationship.

The pattern of doomed passionate lover relationships

Essentially someone with a high light quotient but also carrying a high dark shadow karma in intimate relationships, will tend to attract a partner whose light quotient is low and whose darkness quotient is high. Of course, persons with high darkness quotients are attracted to vibrantly light partners because such relationships fill up their dark emptiness with light and they feel better, without making any personal effort on their own part to become more positive. Lover relationships, particularly with passionate lover relationships, quickly work like a siphon with the higher light quotient person having their light siphoned out to the person with the higher darkness quotient. It is inevitable that in the longer term, the light filled person starts to feel oppressed and less vibrant and less energetic whereas the person high on the darkness quotient starts to feel more energized and more positive about their life. They start to feel happier and healthier while the other party's health, energy and happiness starts to decline.

Pattern of failure in these relationships

These relationships that have large differences in the light quotient can be identified from the outset as high risk and are highly combustible. The foundation of the relationship is based upon one person providing the light source and transmuting the excessive darkness of the other party who chooses not to take any responsibility for their darkness but to live off the light of the high light quotient partner. The high light quotient person may justify their relationship to their friends and others in such terms as: "I'm here to help them become happy", "I find him/her irresistible" or "I just can't live without them". The party high on the darkness quotient may or may not be narcissistic; they may just be unconscious of their own darkness or the burden it places on others. However, they will be aware that at they are highly attracted to the "bright light" partner with whom they have begun a passionate relationship and they: "can't keep their hands off them" and that they feel so much more positive and healthy and energised in the presence of their "bright light" partner.

The overall pattern of long-term unsustainability of these relationships based around the depletion of light from one party by the other is as follows:

Phase: 1: the passionate energetic exchange

Initially, along with the hormonal glue, the exchange of energy is almost addictive. The partner with the high dark quotient starts to feel young again, re-invigorated, happier and more positive about their life which is to be expected as they are receiving light from the person with the high light quotient. The high light quotient person may not initially notice a decline in energy as they are buoyed up by their positive approach to relationships and their desire to love the other person and make them happy. Initially, they cannot do too much to make their lover happy and they experience happiness through feeling needed, and desired. At this point, both partners experience a sense of having found a "soul mate", someone who gives them what they need.

Phase 2: the depletion of the high light quotient person

The person high on the high light quotient is now drained on a daily basis to provide energy to bolster up the quality of the life of the person dominated by the dark quotient and eventually they become exhausted. Over time, often gradually and imperceptibly the high light quotient person starts to experience illnesses they have not had before, and notice that they do not have the same energy level that they once had. This may take six months, a year or two years but eventually particularly after the hormonal boosts die away at two years, the "bright light" will start to feel exhausted and will unconsciously start to seek time for themselves.

Phase 3: withdrawal of their light by the high light quotient person

During phase 3, the high light quotient person starts to withdraw their energy. This is triggered by a number of things, usually exhaustion, or the birth of a baby to whom they now give their full attention, or a new career that interests them, or through personal therapeutic work. Then, they start to place boundaries in between themselves and their high dark quotient lover. This may or may not be conscious but what happens is that they withdraw light /energy from their partner and re-invest it elsewhere. Otherwise, if they do not withdraw energy, they start to collapse into a state of physical or mental ill health. This withdrawal of energy means that the high dark quotient partner starts to feel a collapse in their level of happiness. They no longer have the same level of happiness or vibrant energy that they had earlier in the relationship. Something has changed and they search for a scapegoat.

Phase 4: emergence of the dark shadows

Persons with high dark quotients project their unhappiness upon those closest to them, most often their partner who now becomes the cause of their suffering, that is, the cause of their reduced life energy intake. They may start becoming abusive towards the once "bright light" partner verbally or emotionally. They may accuse them of not giving enough to the relationships, charge them with not living up to the original couple agreement and withdrawing from the relationship. During this phase, dark and nasty interactions increase in intensity, as the once "bright light" may now start to also become reactive, being angry or anxious with increasing frequency. It is now only a matter of time before the relationship self-combusts, unless significant therapeutic work is done and both parties take responsibility for their own happiness. This is unlikely with high dark quotient persons who generally prefer to live in the world as a victim. They blame others for their unhappiness and project their unhappiness onto those nearest and dearest to them with blame, judgment and hatred.

Phase 5: termination patterns in the relationship.

The high light quotient person in the relationships is now bewildered by their partner's criticism and hateful comments and treatment of them. In their best moments they say nothing and suffer within and in their vulnerable moments they strike back, often with tears and anger. They are confused and bewildered as to how they have fallen from grace and why they are now so criticised and disliked. They may go to therapy to try to resolve the problem so that the relationship can continue but unless the therapy is working energetically with these issues, it is unlikely to help. The high light quotient person may have no insight as to why they feel so sick, tired and hopeless and may exit the relationship unconsciously through a cancer or life-terminating illness. Alternatively, they may simply withdraw and focus on other activities in their life or physically leave their partner.

It may be that the dark quotient partner terminates the relationship blaming their partner for not living up to their original agreement, not making them happy or they may stay in the relationship but seek to have affairs with other persons who are also "bright lights" so that they can renew their sources of energy. Alternatively, they may move to a new relationship with someone with the same dark/light quotients as themselves and find that the relationship is sustainable over a long period. It may lack the passion of the relationships with "bright lights" but because from the beginning the dark/light quotients are the same, albeit low, there is no experience of being deprived over time. All remains as it was in the beginning in terms of the levels of light/dark within themselves. They rarely choose to take responsibility for the failure of the relationship or for their own need to change. While the light quotient person is most likely to end the relationship feeling much self-recrimination for "not being good enough", the dark quotient person is most likely to end the relationship feeling a victim, blaming the other person for failing to make them happy.

Case studies:

Mathilda had been in a passionate love relationship with a highly attractive sensual man. She was described by friends as a "bright star", radiant with light and positivity in her day-to-day life prior to meeting her passionate lover who was high on the darkness quotient. Within four years, she was a chronic fatigue case, unable to get out of bed for over six months. She eventually crawled away from the relationship. She blamed herself for not "getting it right" but had no real idea what this meant other than that she could not make him happy despite her best efforts. She noticed that this was a pattern in her life whereby she would give herself devotedly and wholeheartedly to her passionate new lover whose life would turn a positive corner following their meeting. He would start to improve his health physically, become emotionally more positive and his business would start to thrive while she slowly sank into the ground with exhaustion or a string of illnesses. She said it was as though her energy was "sucked out of her in relationships" leaving her as an empty shell while her partner became more positive. Eventually she would become so physically ill that she had no option but to leave the relationship and recover her health and wellbeing for a few years before venturing out again. Unfortunately, without any insight on the problem she had repeated the pattern three times. Each pattern went from passionate love to cinders within a couple of years, always leaving Mathilda ill and depleted while her partners went on to satisfying relationships with women of their own high dark quotient.

Roger was another example. He was sensitive and caring man, and the light radiated from his eyes. Just observing him was sufficient to note that he was high on the "light quotient". He fell passionately in love with a woman high on the dark quotient and despite his faithfulness and devotion to her needs, she started to abuse him verbally and emotionally, claiming that he no longer made her happy. She insisted he care for their three children while she ignored them and had a string of affairs with men around her. She took no responsibility for her neglect of the children or her abuse of Roger. His health declined radically and after six years, he agreed to a divorce with self-recrimination and self-blame. She left the children with him and continued the party life continuing to blame him for not having made her happy.

Managing light/dark quotients in passionate relationships with skilfulness

The single most effective way of managing this light/dark quotient is to choose some-one with the same level of light/dark quotients so that there is no opportunity for relative deprivation over the relationship period. This means essentially that person's who are "bright lights" and high on the light quotient, need to recognise the characteristics of this quality so they can identify it in others. Essentially those high on the light quotient, physically demonstrate this by the bright light in their eyes, their warm smiles, their kind deeds, their compassionate natures and their positive grateful attitude to and appreciation of life. These are the characteristics of the persons whose heart has consistently demonstrated high levels of coherence. They need to become aware of their poor boundaries and of their tendency to make poor relationship choices because their compassion often outweighs their wisdom. They believe that their love can heal those around them and they like to bring light and happiness to those around them. These people need to acquire the wisdom to distinguish between being needed in a relationship because of their "light" versus being in a relationship with an equal light quotient person. They need to develop their ego-sensing skills and learn to identify compatible high light quotient partners. Otherwise, they continue to set themselves up for failure and heartbreak in the intimate relationships for however attractive the initially meeting karmically, the fruits will be bitter. They also must let go of their resolutions, vows, promises and contracts that have come from past lives, that they will bring this person back to the light, or save/heal them in some way. This is the "helper complex" and requires intensive therapeutic work to release as it is an unskilful way of entering into relationships. Although originally this may have come from a deep karmic place in the past of great love and care for that person, today it is no longer an appropriate way of being in intimate relationships.

In contrast, high quotient dark energy persons are characterised by a cluster of characteristics which include some or all of the following: seeing the cup as half empty rather than half full, making others responsible for their happiness, high levels of judgment and blame when they are not feeling happy, failure to take responsibility for their own happiness, seeing themselves as the victim, and narcissistic tendencies or otherwise high levels of self-centredness. These persons face the task of taking responsibility for their own happiness and cultivating their own light. The era of living using another person's light energy is over. It is finished. This is the age of consciousness soul, identified by Steiner so clearly, as the time when every individual must take responsibility for cultivating their own light. It is also the time when all individuals must rise above their immediate sensory passions and desires and engage their consciousness soul, or light generating centre within to make to make skilful decisions within their human relationships.

> *"Let us call what shines forth in the soul as eternal, the consciousness soul. [. . .] The kernel of human consciousness, that is, the soul within the soul, is what is here meant by consciousness soul. The consciousness soul is thus distinguished as a member of the soul distinct from the intellectual soul, which is still entangled in the sensations, impulses and passions. Everyone knows how a man at first counts as true what he prefers in his feelings and desires. Only that truth is permanent, however, that has freed itself from all flavour of such sympathy and antipathy of feeling. The truth is true even if all personal feelings revolt against it. That part of the soul in which this truth lives will be called consciousness soul."*
>
> *Steiner, R Theosophy https://zooey.wordpress.com/2010/10/22/consciousness-soul/*

For different reasons, both high dark quotient lovers and high light quotient lovers, must cultivate and develop consciousness soul so they may become capable of creating skilful intimate relationships.

In this era with opportunities for a number of intimate lover relationships in a single lifetime, it is humbling to remember that they are the greatest mirror, other than our own children, in which to view our own fragilities and shadows. Conversely, they provide splendid opportunities for personal growth and development as they make visible that, which is largely invisible in our own single worlds. For this alone, gratitude for the opportunity to learn through passionate intimate lover relationships is essential.

References

Hawkins, D (1995) *Power vs Force: The Hidden Determinants of Human Behaviour* Hay House, California.

McCraty, R.,Atkinson, M.,Tomasino, D. and Bradley,R. (2006) *The coherent Heart, Heart–Brain Interactions, Psychophysiological Coherence, and the Emergence of System-Wide Orde*r Institute of Heartmath, Boulder, Colorado.

Sachedeva, S (2012) *The eight spiritual breaths*. Yogi impressions, Mumbai

Steiner, R *Theosophy* https://zooey.wordpress.com/2010/10/22/consciousness-soul/ (accessed 27-9-16).

www.ingramcontent.com/pod-product-compliance
Lightning Source LLC
Chambersburg PA
CBHW040321300426
44112CB00020B/2833